Child Abuse

Series Editor: Cara Acred

Volume 320

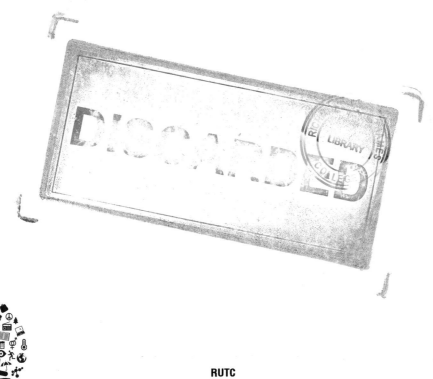

Independence Educational Publishers

First published by Independence Educational Publishers

The Studio, High Green

Great Shelford

Cambridge CB22 5EG

England

© Independence 2017

Copyright

Photocopy licence

ISBN-13: 978 1 86168 772 2

Printed in Great Britain

Zenith Print Group

Contents

Introduction

CHILD ABUSE is Volume 320 in the **ISSUES** series. The aim of the series is to offer current, diverse information about important issues in our world, from a UK perspective.

ABOUT TITLE

Child protection and child abuse are extremely difficult topics to address. This book looks at the issues of child exploitation, female genital mutilation and neglect as well as child marriage. It also considers safeguarding topics such as abuse in sports and looks at how we can better protect young people against these kinds of dangers.

OUR SOURCES

Titles in the **ISSUES** series are designed to function as educational resource books, providing a balanced overview of a specific subject.

The information in our books is comprised of facts, articles and opinions from many different sources, including:

⇨ Newspaper reports and opinion pieces

⇨ Website factsheets

⇨ Magazine and journal articles

⇨ Statistics and surveys

⇨ Government reports

⇨ Literature from special interest groups.

A NOTE ON CRITICAL EVALUATION

Because the information reprinted here is from a number of different sources, readers should bear in mind the origin of the text and whether the source is likely to have a particular bias when presenting information (or when conducting their research). It is hoped that, as you read about the many aspects of the issues explored in this book, you will critically evaluate the information presented.

It is important that you decide whether you are being presented with facts or opinions. Does the writer give a biased or unbiased report? If an opinion is being expressed, do you agree with the writer? Is there potential bias to the 'facts' or statistics behind an article?

ASSIGNMENTS

In the back of this book, you will find a selection of assignments designed to help you engage with the articles you have been reading and to explore your own opinions. Some tasks will take longer than others and there is a mixture of design, writing and research-based activities that you can complete alone or in a group.

Useful weblinks

www.abuselaw.co.uk

www.barnardos.org.uk

www.blueknot.org.au

www.britishcouncil.org

www.crae.org.uk

www.theconversation.com

www.dur.ac.uk

www.fullfact.org

www.theguardian.com

www.highspeedtraining.co.uk

www.independent.co.uk

www.nhs.uk

www.nurseryworld.co.uk

www.victimsupport.org.uk

www.ucl.ac.uk

www.untribune.com

FURTHER RESEARCH

At the end of each article we have listed its source and a website that you can visit if you would like to conduct your own research. Please remember to critically evaluate any sources that you consult and consider whether the information you are viewing is accurate and unbiased.

Childhood abuse

Child abuse can happen in different ways, and can include neglect as well as physical, emotional and sexual abuse. In many cases, people experience more than one type of abuse.

Often, people abuse others because they want power and control over them. If you were abused as a child, it's important to remember that it's not your fault or because of anything that you did. Abusive behaviour towards children is always wrong and never the child's fault.

We know that around one in four adults, both male and female, has experienced abuse as a child. Some find that with the support of their family and friends they are able to move on from their childhood abuse. But for many survivors, talking about the abuse to someone who is professional, caring and independent, from an organisation that helps survivors, such as Victim Support, is an essential step. We can help you to develop the coping strategies you may need to manage the overwhelming feelings that the impact of childhood abuse can have in adulthood.

Impact of childhood abuse

Everyone is different. It's not easy to know exactly how you will feel as an adult living with past experiences of being abused. You may have reported the abuse as a child, lived with it in secret for years, or only recently remembered the abuse you experienced. However, it's possible that at some time in your adult life your memories or fears will come back, which can lead to some very intense emotions.

Different life experiences can trigger these emotions, including bereavement, becoming a parent, experiencing an unrelated crime, moving to a new area, and current news stories in the media.

Emotional health

Not everybody who has experienced childhood abuse will also experience emotional or mental health difficulties. However, it's estimated that over 50% of people may have the following symptoms that last into adulthood:

⇨ anxiety

⇨ depression

⇨ post-traumatic stress

⇨ sleep disorders

⇨ self-harm and/or suicidal thoughts.

Physical health

Childhood abuse is associated with poorer physical health in adulthood. You may find it more difficult to go to your local GP, hospital or dentist to get help for general medical issues or a check-up because of not wanting to be touched or asked questions.

Struggling to cope

Some people find it very difficult to deal with the intimate aspects of childhood abuse, especially when they have to talk to other people about what happened. They may have kept their experiences secret for years and are worried about the effect that 'going public' will have on their family and other people around them.

If you were abused by someone you know or love, the effects may be even greater. As well as the experience itself, you've had your trust broken at an early point in your life; this can have lasting negative effects on your relationships with other people and be a barrier to developing a positive sexual identity.

Abuse in childhood can also leave you feeling very confused; you may be questioning your own memories of the abuse, or wondering if you could have done something to stop what happened. It's important to remember that you were a child and the abuser manipulated you in order to harm you.

Survivors may also feel guilty because as a result of abuse, they have engaged in risk taking or unhealthy behaviours. These may include alcohol or substance abuse, criminal activity or avoiding medical help. These are common responses to childhood abuse, and support services will understand this and help you develop more positive coping strategies.

What can I do?

Childhood abuse can be particularly difficult to deal with on your own. Some things you can do are:

⇨ Talk to someone you trust. Many survivors find that talking to a specialist agency or independent person, such as a GP, is a first step to understanding what has happened, and working out how to move forward. You can also talk to Victim Support for free and confidential support, regardless of whether you have reported the abuse.

⇨ Survivor forums, such as the NAPAC website, enable you to share your story anonymously with other survivors.

⇨ Get help for any specific issues, such as drug and alcohol misuse, offending behaviours, or parenting challenges. The professionals who work in these areas will be experienced in supporting survivors of childhood abuse, and will be able to give you the expert help that you need.

⇨ Report the abuse to the police. Even though it may have been many years since the abuse happened, the police are trained to respond sensitively and to take all disclosures of childhood abuse seriously. Read the *Victim Reporting Factsheet* to learn how to report abuse and what will happen next.

➡ If your abuse happened within an organisation or institution (such as schools, children's homes, hospitals or charities) where you should have been protected as a child, you can get help from the Independent Inquiry into Child Sexual Abuse. The inquiry will also examine cases of child sexual abuse involving well-known people in the media, politics and other areas of public life.

How Victim Support can help

We believe that everyone who has experienced childhood abuse should be able to get the help they need, and the support that will empower them to recover from the impact of abuse. We don't just help people who've recently been abused – we are here to support both men and women weeks, months and years after the abuse took place.

We have different services in different parts of the country. All of our services are confidential, free and available to anyone who's been abused. We can help, regardless of whether you have told the police or anyone else about the abuse.

Our ISVA (Independent Sexual Violence Advocates) services are staffed by specialist caseworkers and supported by specialist volunteers. They'll help you to decide what action you want to take and the support and help that feels right for you. ISVAs often support survivors through the criminal justice system, and co-ordinate health and support services.

Our victims' services teams work with anyone affected by crime. They'll help you decide on the range of support and help that might benefit you.

Confidentiality

We will work with you in a confidential way. This means that we will not share any information with your family, the police or anyone else without your permission. The only time we will ever share any information without your permission is if we are worried about a child or vulnerable person's safety.

We may be worried that if you tell us about an adult who abused you as a child, they may be in a position where they have abused, or are still abusing, another person. We will always explain to you our boundaries of confidentiality and talk to you about how we can best share information with the police if necessary, while helping to keep you safe.

Get in touch: Victim Support can help

When you report a crime to the police, they should automatically ask you if you would like help from an organisation like Victim Support. But anyone affected by crime can contact us directly if they want to – you don't need to talk to the police to get our help.

You can contact us by:

➡ Requesting support online

➡ Contacting your local Victim Support team

➡ Calling our Supportline for free on 08 08 16 89 111 or emailing us

If English is not your first language and you would like some support, call our Supportline and let us know which language you speak, and we will call you back with an interpreter as soon as possible. We also welcome calls via Next Generation Text on 18001 08 08 16 89 111.

Families and friends affected by crime can also contact us for support and information. If you're a child or young person under 18 and are looking for support, visit our You & Co website, where we have lots of information and tips specifically for children and young people.

➡ The above information is reprinted with kind permission from Victim Support. Please visit www.victimsupport.org.uk for further information.

© Victim Support 2017

Number and types of child abuse that survivors experienced before the age of 16, by sex, year ending March 2016	
	Percentage
1 type of abuse	58
Psychological abuse only	14
Physical abuse only	10
Any sexual assault only	19
Witnessed domestic violence or abuse only	15
2 types of abuse	23
Psychological abuse & physical abuse	7
Psychological abuse & any sexual assault	3
Psychological abuse & witnessed domestic violence or abuse	6
Physical abuse & any sexual assault	2
Physical abuse & witnessed domestic violence or abuse	3
Any sexual assault & witnessed domestic violence or abuse	3

Source: Abuse during childhood: findings from the Crime Survey for England and Wales, year ending March 2016, Office for National Statistics, 4 August 2016

The scale of abuse during childhood: how much do we know?

In brief

Claim

1. One in 14 adults was abused as a child in England and Wales. BBC News, 4 August 2016

2. Six million adults were abused as children in England and Wales. *The Times*, 5 August 2016

Conclusion

1. This refers to sexual abuse and is roughly correct according to estimates from the Crime Survey.

2. This is correct according to estimates from the Crime Survey.

Although it's not obvious, the headlines above are actually talking about different things, while accurately reporting the figures.

About six million adults – aged 16 to 59 in England and Wales – are estimated by the Office for National Statistics to have experienced abuse as children.

Meanwhile an estimated two million adults of the same age range experienced sexual abuse specifically as children. That's either one in 14 or one in 15 depending on how you round the figures.

How do we now know these things, and how much should we trust the numbers?

Asking people about their experiences

All the figures are based on a survey which asks adults to recall any experiences of abuse when they were children. It formed part of the Crime Survey for England and Wales last year.

This is obviously a sensitive topic, so rather than interview people in their homes about their experiences (which is how most of the Crime Survey works), people are handed a tablet by the interviewer and complete the questions themselves. The interviewer can't see their answers. This is also how we get estimates of things like illegal drug use, domestic violence and sexual assault.

Even so, the ONS says that the figures probably undercount sexual abuse, since some people will either not recall or not wish to recall events from their past.

In addition, the statisticians point out that social norms are different now to what they were several decades ago, which may affect the way people of different ages report their experiences.

What is meant by 'abuse'

Four kinds of abuse are being measured here: physical, psychological and sexual abuse, and witnessing domestic abuse (which has been found to cause harm in itself). Abuse by other children – for instance bullying at school – isn't included.

Each of these is defined in detail by the Survey. Psychological abuse, for example, is defined as when people indicate they were:

"… not loved; told that they should never have been born; threatened to be abandoned or thrown out of the family home; repeatedly belittled to the extent that they felt worthless; physically threatened or someone close to them physically threatened, and emotionally neglected."

An estimated six million adults experienced any one or more of these four kinds of abuse during childhood, according to the Survey. The estimate for sexual abuse was just over two million.

Women were significantly more likely than men to report experience of abuse during childhood. The biggest difference was for sexual abuse: 11% of women reported some form of experience compared to 3% of men.

Older people were also more likely to report abuse than younger generations. Over 20% of people aged 45–59 reported some form of abuse, compared to 14% aged 16–24.

We can't tell from this evidence whether this means abuse in childhood is falling over time, or if it just means that people are more willing to disclose abuse the older they get and the further they are from the experience.

10 August 2016

⇨ The above information is reprinted with kind permission from Full Fact. Please visit www.fullfact.org for further information.

Types of child abuse

Child abuse and neglect occur in different situations, for a range of reasons. Children rarely experience one form of abuse at a time. Recent research by McGill University (2015) showed that emotional abuse of a child may be as harmful as physical abuse and neglect, while child sexual abuse often occurs together with other forms of maltreatment.

Emotional abuse

Emotional abuse or maltreatment, also known as psychological abuse or maltreatment is the most common form of child abuse. It is also experienced by children witnessing domestic violence. While many parents are emotionally abusive without being violent or sexually abusive, emotional abuse often accompanies physical and sexual abuse. It includes acts of omission (what is not done), e.g. emotional neglect, not expressing or showing love and affection, and commission (what is done), e.g. rejection, humiliation, insults, setting unreasonable expectations or restricting opportunities for the child to learn, socialise or explore. Each can negatively impact a child's self-esteem and social competence.

Some parents do not see the child as a separate person, and fulfil their own needs and goals, rather than their children's. Their parenting style may be aggressive, and include shouting and intimidation. They may isolate or confine the child, or they may manipulate their children using more subtle means, such as emotional blackmail. Emotional abuse and neglect were the primary reason for a child being investigated for maltreatment in 2014–15 (AIHW, 2016).

Emotional abuse does not only occur in the home. Children can be emotionally abused by teachers, other adults in a position of power and other children in the form of 'bullying'. Chronic emotional abuse in schools is a serious cause of harm and warrants ongoing active intervention.

What are the characteristics of emotionally abusive parents?

Some parents who have their own unresolved trauma can find parenting challenging, and have difficulties with attachment, emotional regulation, boundaries and discipline. Emotional abuse has increasingly been linked to parental mental health problems, domestic violence, drug and alcohol misuse, being abused or having been in care as children (Iwaneic and Herbert, 1999; Siegel and Hartzell, 2003). Research findings suggest that some emotionally abusive parents have negative attitudes towards children, perceive parenting as unrewarding and difficult to enjoy, and that they associate their own negative feelings with the child's difficult behaviour, particularly when the child reacts against their poor parenting methods.

Signs in childhood

From infancy to adulthood, emotionally abused people are often more withdrawn and emotionally disengaged than their peers, and find it difficult to predict other people's behaviour, understand why they behave in the manner that they do, and respond appropriately.

Emotionally abused children exhibit a range of specific signs. They often: feel unhappy, frightened and distressed,

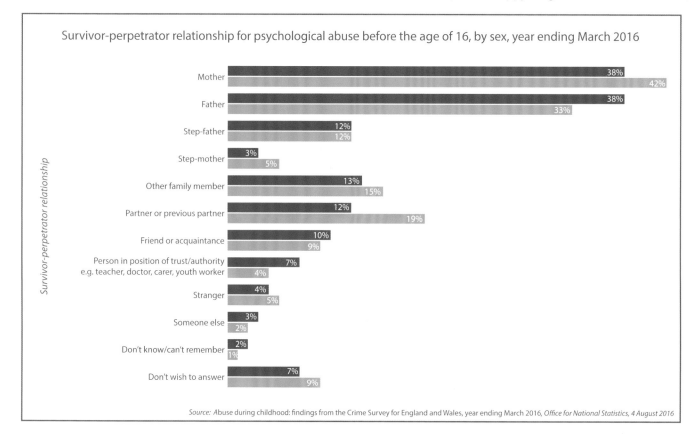

Survivor-perpetrator relationship for psychological abuse before the age of 16, by sex, year ending March 2016

Survivor-perpetrator relationship

Relationship	
Mother	38% / 42%
Father	38% / 33%
Step-father	12% / 12%
Step-mother	3% / 5%
Other family member	13% / 15%
Partner or previous partner	12% / 19%
Friend or acquaintance	10% / 9%
Person in position of trust/authority e.g. teacher, doctor, carer, youth worker	7% / 4%
Stranger	4% / 5%
Someone else	3% / 2%
Don't know/can't remember	2% / 1%
Don't wish to answer	7% / 9%

Source: Abuse during childhood: findings from the Crime Survey for England and Wales, year ending March 2016, Office for National Statistics, 4 August 2016

behave aggressively and antisocially or too maturely for their age, experience difficulties with school attendance and achievement, find it hard to make friends, show signs of physical neglect and malnourishment, experience incontinence and mysterious pains.

Signs in adulthood

Adults emotionally abused as children are more likely to experience mental health problems and difficulties in personal relationships. Many of the harms of physical and sexual abuse are related to the emotional abuse that accompanies them, and as a result many emotionally abused adults exhibit a range of complex psychological and psychosocial problems associated with multiple forms of trauma in childhood (Glaser, 2002).

Significant early relationships in childhood shape our response to new social situations in adulthood. Adults with emotionally abusive parents are at a disadvantage as they try to form personal, professional and romantic relationships, since they may easily misinterpret other people's behaviours and social cues, or misapply the rules that governed their abusive relationship with their parent to everyday social situations (Berenson and Anderson, 2006).

Neglect

Neglect can be defined as "any serious act or omission by a person having the care of a child that, within the bounds of cultural tradition, constitutes a failure to provide conditions that are essential for the healthy physical and emotional development of a child" (CFCA Resource Sheet, 2016). Notifications of neglect constitute a significant proportion of referrals to child protection services. Neglect refers to circumstances in which a parent or caregiver fails to adequately provide for a child's needs: e.g. provision of food, shelter and clothing, access to medical care when necessary, providing love, care and support, adequate supervision, appropriate legal and moral guidance, regular school attendance.

Sometimes, a parent might not be physically or mentally able to care for

a child. This may occur as a result of their own illness, injury, depression, anxiety or substance abuse. Neglect can sometimes be associated with socioeconomic status. Many parents don't have the resources to meet a child's need. Their financial hardship might also put them into contact with welfare services, which scrutinise their parenting practices, and so, are more likely to make a report. This has meant that poor families and communities have previously been stigmatised; however, it is important to recognise that emotional abuse and neglect occur in all families, rich or poor.

There are several categories of neglect: supervisory neglect, emotional neglect, physical neglect, medical neglect, educational neglect and abandonment (Scott, 2014).

Signs in childhood (these signs are similar to those for emotional abuse) are dependent on the age of the child. Babies and young children may not seem to have a close relationship to their parent or caregiver, may be overly anxious and lack confidence, may be aggressive or overly affectionate to strangers and people they don't know well. Older children may speak or act inappropriately for their age, be socially isolated, including isolated from their parents, have few social skills, and struggle to control their intense emotions or outbursts.

Physical abuse

Physical abuse refers to "any non-accidental physical act inflicted upon a child by a person having the care of a child". It is not always a result of intent to hurt a child but sometimes can be justified as being a form of discipline. However, when it is fear-based, and involves unpredictability or lashing out in anger, it constitutes physical abuse. Physical abuse is the type of abuse most likely to be accompanied by another form, specifically emotional abuse or neglect. When a parent or caregiver 'makes up' an illness it is also considered physical abuse (Bromfield, 2005; World Health Organization [WHO], 2006).

Adults who physically abuse children

may have unrealistic expectations of their child, not understanding the child's needs or how to interact with them. This can be fuelled by their own health, relationship, child abuse histories or manifest with emotional or behavioural challenges including anger management issues (Miller-Perrin and Perrin, 2013).

Overall, physical abuse has been a normal aspect of domestic life in Australia for a long time. Physical assaults that would be serious criminal offenses if committed by one man against another – for instance, hitting, slapping, or striking with an object – have been legally and socially sanctioned when committed by a man against his wife and child, or by parents against their children. Today, incidents of domestic violence committed against both women and children remain at epidemic proportions, although there is increasing recognition within the Australian community of the prevalence and harms of violence against women and children.

Whilst community attitudes to violence against women and children have changed for the better, Australian policy-makers have failed to outlaw physical assaults against children by caregivers. According to the 2007 report of the Global Initiative to End All Corporal Punishment of Children, Australia is one of a number of countries that has failed to prohibit violence against children, and has failed to commit to legislative reform. In particular, the legal defences of 'reasonable correction' and 'reasonable chastisement' are still available to adults who are charged with violent offenses against children in many jurisdictions.

Signs in childhood

Physically abused children find it difficult relating to their peers and the adults around them. The constant threat of violence at home makes them perpetually vigilant and mistrustful, and they may be overly domineering and aggressive in their attempts to predict and control other people's behaviour. They are also vulnerable to 'emotional storms', or instances of overwhelming emotional responses to everyday situations (Berenson and Anderson 2006). These 'storms' can

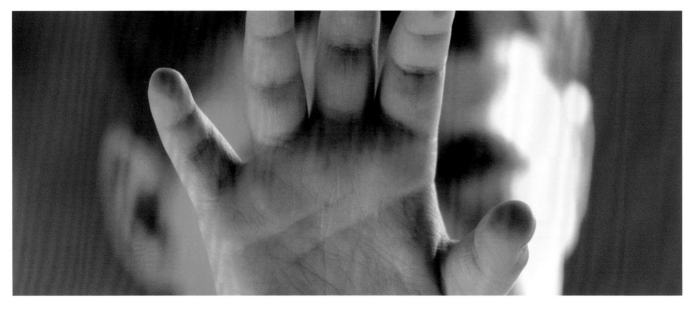

take the form of profound grief, fear or rage.

Physically abused children may also have problems with academic achievement, physical development and coordination, developing friendships and relationships, aggression and anger management, depression, anxiety and low self-esteem.

Signs in adulthood

Adults physically abused in childhood are at increased risk of either aggressive and violent behaviour, or shy and avoidant behaviour leading to rejection or re-victimisation. This polarised behaviour is often driven by hyper-vigilance and the anticipation of threat and violence even in everyday situations. Men with a history of physical abuse in childhood are particularly prone to violent behaviour, and physically abused men are over-represented amongst violent and sexual offenders (Malinosky-Rummell and Hansen 1993).

Domestic and family violence

Domestic and family violence is a pattern of abusive behaviour in an intimate relationship, which features coercion and control, that over time puts one person in a position of power over another and causes fear. It can incorporate a range of abuses including but not limited to: physical, sexual and emotional assaults; stalking;

isolating the person from friends and family; financial abuse; spiritual/cultural abuse; legal abuse; damage to personal property; threats of harm to pets and loved ones; psychological abuse, e.g. manipulation, denial, etc.

Women are more likely to experience violence from intimate partners than men; they can also experience violence from ex-partners. It does need to be noted, however, that women can and do commit violent offences in families although not as commonly as males. It occurs in all cultures, religions, socio-demographic groups and any sort of intimate relationship. It is particularly damaging to children who either experience or witness it.

Signs in childhood

Children living in a family violence environment are living in a situation of fear, anxiety and unpredictability. They experience emotional and psychological trauma similar to children experiencing other forms of child abuse and neglect. Some will be directly targeted and may experience physical or sexual abuse as well as neglect.

A child witnessing family violence is at risk of: behavioural and emotional difficulties, learning difficulties, long-term developmental problems, aggressive language and behaviour, restlessness, anxiety and depression.

Signs in adulthood

Adults exposed to domestic violence as children can carry with them a legacy of trauma-related symptoms and developmental delays. Women

who grew up in an environment of family violence are more likely to be victimised in adulthood, whilst men who grew up in a violent environment are more likely to commit violent offences in adulthood (World Health Organization, 'World Report on Violence and Health', ed. by Krug, Etienne G., et al., Geneva, 2002).

Sexual abuse

Child sexual abuse describes any incident, in which an adult, adolescent or child uses their power and authority to engage a minor in a sexual act, or exposes the minor to inappropriate sexual behaviour or material. A person may sexually abuse a child using threats and physical force, but sexual abuse often involves subtle forms of manipulation, in which the child is coerced into believing that the activity is an expression of love, or that the child brought the abuse upon themselves. Sexual abuse involves contact and non-contact offences.

Sexually abusive behaviours can include the fondling of genitals, masturbation, oral sex, vaginal or anal penetration by a penis, finger or any other object, fondling of breasts, voyeurism, exhibitionism and exposing the child to or involving the child in pornography (CFCA Resource Sheet, 2015: Bromfield, 2005; US National Research Council, 1993).

How many children are sexually abused?

Up to eight per cent of males and

12 per cent of females experience penetrative child sexual abuse and up to 16 per cent of males and up to 36 per cent of females experience non-penetrative child sexual abuse (Price-Robertson, Bromfield & Vassallo, 2010). Adult retrospective studies show that one in four women and one in six men were sexually abused before the age of 18 (Centre for Disease Control and Prevention, 2006).

Who is most likely to be sexually abused?

Whilst all children are vulnerable to sexual abuse, girls are more likely to be sexually abused than boys. Disabled children are up to seven times more likely to be abused than their non-disabled peers (Briggs, 2006).

Who sexually abuses children?

Most sexual abusers are male although females also do perpetrate abuse (McCloskey & Raphael, 2005). Some offenders are serial perpetrators – high risk, others opportunistic (due to lack of control) and some situational (Irenyi, Bromfield, Beyer, & Higgins, 2006). Most adults who sexually abuse children are not mentally ill and do not meet the diagnostic criteria for 'paedophilia' i.e. are sexually attracted to children.

Signs in childhood

Sexually abused children exhibit a range of behaviours, including: withdrawn, unhappy and suicidal behaviour; self-harm and suicidality; aggressive and violent behaviour; bedwetting, sleep problems, nightmares; eating problems, e.g. anorexia nervosa and bulimia nervosa; mood swings; detachment; pains for no medical reason; sexual behaviour, language or knowledge too advanced for their age

Signs in adulthood

Adults sexually abused as children often experience poorer mental and physical health than other adults (Draper et al., 2007). They are more likely to have a history of eating disorders, anxiety, depression and other mental health issues, substance abuse, self-harm and suicide attempts. Sexual abuse is also associated with difficulties in interpersonal relationships, self-esteem, completing an education and maintaining employment.

Organised sexual abuse

Organised sexual abuse refers to the range of circumstances in which multiple children are subject to sexual abuse by multiple perpetrators. In these circumstances, children are subject to a range of serious harms that can include child prostitution, the manufacture of child pornography, and bizarre and sadistic sexual practices, including ritualistic abuse and torture (Salter M., 2012).

What are the circumstances in which children are subject to organised sexual abuse?

Many children subject to organised abuse are raised in abusive families, and their parents make them available for abuse outside the home. This abuse may include extended family members, family 'friends' or people who pay to abuse the child (Cleaver and Freeman, 1996). Other children are trafficked into organised abuse by perpetrators in schools, churches, state or religious institutions, or whilst homeless or without stable housing.

Who is most likely to be sexually abused in organised contexts?

Children who are vulnerable to organised abuse include the children of parents involved in organised abuse, and children from unstable or unhappy family backgrounds who may be targeted by abusers outside the family.

Who sexually abuses children in organised contexts?

Organised abuse, like all forms of child abuse, is primarily committed by parents and relatives. Organised abuse differs from other forms of sexual abuse in that women are often reported as perpetrators. Research with female sexual abusers has found that they have often grown up in environments, such as organised abuse, where sexual abuse is normative, and, as adults, they may sexually abuse in organised contexts alongside male offenders (Faller, 1995).

Signs in childhood

Young children subject to organised sexual abuse often have severe traumatic and dissociative symptoms that inhibit disclosure or help-seeking behaviour. They are often very withdrawn children with strong suicidal ideation. They may exhibit disturbed behaviours while at play or when socialising with their peers or other adults.

Signs in adulthood

Organised abuse, and ritual abuse, is a key predisposing factor in the development of Dissociative Identity Disorder and other dissociative spectrum disorders. Adults with histories of organised abuse frequently have long histories of suicide attempts and self-harm, and they often live with a heavy burden of mental and physical disability.

⇨   The above information is reprinted with kind permission from the Blue Knot Foundation. Please visit www.blueknot.org.au for further information.

Understanding why children may stay quiet about abuse

By Louise Petty

It's impossible to put an exact number on how many children in the UK are suffering from abuse at any one time as so many cases go undetected or are never reported. The NSPCC states that there are currently over 56,000 children identified as needing protection from abuse in the UK, yet this doesn't represent the full story.

It's actually predicted that for every child needing protection from abuse, another eight are suffering in silence. This could put the actual figure nearer to half a million children.

But why do so many children never speak out about the abuse they are suffering? There are plenty of places that children can turn to for help, whether it's their parents, a teacher, a family friend or a service like ChildLine. And whilst it's true that some children do willingly disclose information about what's happening to them, the majority will never say anything, or at least not at the time. A 2013 report by the NSPCC found that it takes 7.8 years (on average) for a child to open up to someone about sexual abuse.

Why do some children stay quiet about abuse?

Despite there being a range of people for children to talk to, it's evident that many child victims choose to keep their experiences of abuse hidden. This could be for a variety of reasons and isn't simply because keeping secrets is something that children and teenagers 'just do'. Children may keep quiet about abuse for various reasons:

They may feel guilty or to blame

Children may blame themselves for what's going on and may feel too guilty or ashamed to tell someone. They may think that the abuse is their fault because they've done something to deserve it. As a result, the details of what's happening may feel too embarrassing for them to talk about, making it easier for them to simply say nothing.

They may love the abuser and think the abuse is normal

If the child is being abused by someone that they know, trust and love – a friend or family member – then they may believe that the abuse is normal and not recognise that anything is wrong. They may believe that they're in control of the situation because they have a positive relationship with the person in question.

They may be afraid of the consequences

Children often hold back from telling someone about the abuse they're suffering because they're scared of what might happen next. They may worry that they'll get in trouble (with the person they've told or with the abuser) or that they'll get the abuser in trouble for 'telling on them'. The child may also be concerned about the adult's reaction – that they'll be angry, frightened or shocked, that they may go to the police or that they'll have the child put into care.

They may worry that they won't be believed

It can take a lot of courage for a child to approach an adult and disclose information about abuse, so it's understandable that the child may choose not to say anything just in case the adult doesn't believe what they are being told. The child may prefer to keep quiet rather than risk being humiliated, ignored or dismissed.

They may not have the ability to speak out

Younger children, or those who have a disability, may not have the words to describe what is happening to them, let alone the ability to understand what is going on. Children are vulnerable at any age but particularly so if they don't have the skills to recognise the abuse. This can easily lead to cases of abuse going undetected.

They may be hoping that the abuse will stop

A child may refrain from speaking out about the abuse they are suffering because they believe that the situation is only temporary and that it will soon stop. The child may think they are being punished for something, or that the abuse is just a part of normal life, and may be waiting for the moment to pass.

They have never been asked

In some cases it may be that the child is simply waiting for someone to notice that something isn't right. The child may not have the courage or opportunity to speak out and they may be hoping that a trusted adult will approach them and ask what's wrong. This makes it essential for adults to stay alert to the possible signs of abuse and discuss the behaviours with the child when appropriate.

What to do if you suspect a child is being abused

It's evident that many child victims of abuse will never say anything about what is happening to them. In some cases, children do try and speak out, but the person they've chosen to talk to simply doesn't listen. And this can have quite an impact – if the child has tried to say something and been ignored, why would they bother trying again?

If you ever have any worries about a child then it's important that you act on your concerns straight away. Try talking to the child if you feel it's appropriate and report your concerns to a Designated Safeguarding Officer, social services, the police or the NSPCC.

Always record any physical signs of injury on a Child Protection Body Map for future reference.

It's always better to act and learn that your concerns were only speculation than ignore the warning signs and find that something terrible has happened to a child.

17 May 2016

⇨ The above information is reprinted with kind permission from High Speed Training Ltd. Please visit www.highspeedtraining.co.uk for further information.

It's not on the radar

The hidden diversity of children and young people at risk of sexual exploitation in England. Executive summary.

Child sexual exploitation (CSE) can affect all children – including those with disabilities – regardless of gender identity, sexuality, ethnicity, faith or economic background. Nevertheless, public and professional perception often stereotypes victims of CSE as white girls from disadvantaged backgrounds who are assumed to be heterosexual. While some victims and children at risk do meet this description, assumptions can prevent the identification of other children who do not fit the stereotype.

In 2015, a series of four round tables was held with experts in the fields of CSE and diversity to discuss how the two areas connect. The round tables focused on:

⇨ boys and young men

⇨ lesbian, gay, bisexual, trans and questioning (LGBTQ) young people

⇨ disability[1]

⇨ ethnicity and faith.

Bringing together the findings of the round table events and additional research, *It's not on the radar* explores how perceptions of sexual exploitation can affect the identification of and response to CSE.[2]

Understanding CSE and the different methods that perpetrators use to exploit must be considered in parallel with the fact that children are not defined by one aspect of their identity. A victim of sexual exploitation may have multiple identities and, for example, be male, gay, come from a faith group that does not tolerate homosexuality and have a

---

1 Learning/developmental disabilities and learning difficulties were also included in the umbrella term 'disability', although it is recognised that this includes many different conditions.

2 This report does not attempt to cover all aspects of diversity and recognises that other issues may not be addressed.

disability. What makes a young person vulnerable to sexual exploitation is very individual, and while an identity alone may not result in vulnerability, all aspects of a child's identity must be considered when identifying and raising awareness of CSE.

Due to the complex identities of individuals, there are many themes that cut across all four areas. For example:

⇨ A young person's chronological age may be different from their developmental age, or apparently at odds with their experience of relationships, for example if they have a learning disability or come out as LGBT in their late teens or early twenties.

⇨ Young people and professionals may normalise abuse experienced through CSE, either because of lack of knowledge about CSE or because it is viewed as 'normal' for, or by, the network or group the young person has been exploited in.

⇨ The lack of sex and relationships education affects all young people, regardless of their identity, although some children – such as those with learning disabilities or those who are LGBTQ – are less likely to receive any, or relevant, sex and relationships education.

There are a number of factors that are relevant to particular 'groups' of children and young people addressed in this report.

Key findings

Boys and young men:

⇨ Societal values regarding masculinity and perceptions of males as perpetrators are seen to mask the fact that boys and young men can be victims too.

⇨ Males seem to find it particularly hard to disclose abuse.

⇨ Fear of being labelled gay,

particularly in communities where there is homophobia, can prevent disclosure.

⇨ There is too little recognition of the fact that a male can be both a victim and a perpetrator.

⇨ Boys can be sexually exploited by peers, particularly in gang situations.

⇨ Research has found that male and female CSE victims share certain common traits but also exhibit significant differences in terms of, for example, disability and youth offending rates.[3]

⇨ It might be assumed that young men engaging in sex are doing so because they are highly sexualised, gay or bisexual, and not because they are being exploited.

Lesbian, gay, bisexual, trans and questioning (LGBTQ) young people:

⇨ LGBTQ young people may feel isolated and believe there will be a lack of acceptance by other people regarding their sexuality and gender identity. They may seek support via adult-orientated groups, online or, in the case of boys and young men, in public sex environments such as 'cottages' or 'cruising grounds'.

⇨ There is little in the way of educational resources or general information that provides advice to LGBTQ young people about what a healthy relationship is.

⇨ Societal attitudes towards sexual relationships among lesbian, gay, bisexual and trans people can result in unhealthy or unsafe sexual relationships being accepted as 'normal'.

⇨ Professionals should only share information about a young person's sexuality and gender identity if the young person has agreed that they can do this. Agreement should also be reached on those individuals with whom this information may be shared.

⇨ Possible sexual exploitation in lesbian and trans relationships should be given equal consideration as sexual exploitation within male gay relationships.

⇨ LGBT communities might be reluctant to talk about or acknowledge CSE for fear of exacerbating homo/bi/transphobia.

Ethnicity and faith:

⇨ Community and faith groups are not homogenous and there can be a diversity of cultural and religious practices within communities.

⇨ Victims of sexual exploitation come from all ethnic backgrounds, regardless of how conservative or 'protected' children may appear.

⇨ Cultural and religious views and practices, particularly those that prize a female's virginity or a male's heterosexuality, may prevent victims from speaking out due to a fear of retribution or rejection from families.

⇨ Access to communities should be via a broad range of stakeholders, rather than solely through male religious leaders, and particularly through those with child-centred perspectives.

⇨ Working with groups that are committed to child protection and to opposing violence and abuse, such as women's organisations and others not often associated with CSE, could enable better identification of victims.

Disabilities:

⇨ Children and young people with a disability are three times more likely to be abused than children without a disability.[4] Within this group, children with behaviour or conduct disorders are particularly vulnerable.

⇨ Children and young people

with disabilities are often over-protected and not informed about sex and relationships.

⇨ The transition from children's services into independent living is a particularly vulnerable time for young people with disabilities.

⇨ Learning difficulties or delayed development may be a consequence of trauma or sexual abuse.

⇨ A lack of diagnosis and assessment for learning disabilities can result in a child's behaviour being misunderstood, and exclusion from school. This can lead to the child being vulnerable to CSE.

The true scale of sexual exploitation is unknown, and it is recognised that while not all children and young people will be victims, all must be given the confidence and resilience to identify risky relationships and develop healthy ones. No child is ever to blame for their abuse, regardless of their actions, and adults must be aware of the issue and confident to identify and respond, regardless of the sexuality and gender identity, ethnicity, faith or disability of the child concerned.

2016

⇨ The above information is reprinted with kind permission from Barnardo's. Please visit www. barnardos.org.uk for further information,

3 Cockbain, E; Brayley, H; Ashby, M (2014) Not just a girl thing: A large-scale comparison of male and female users of child sexual exploitation services in the UK.

4 Miller, D; Brown, J (2014) 'We have the right to be safe': Protecting disabled children from abuse.

Spotting signs of child sexual abuse

One in 20 children in the UK will experience child sexual abuse. Here are the signs to be aware of and what to do if you suspect a child is being sexually abused.

What is child sexual abuse?

Child sexual abuse is illegal in the UK and covers a range of sexual activities, including:

⇨ possessing images of child pornography

⇨ forcing a child to strip or masturbate

⇨ engaging in any kind of sexual activity in front of a child, including watching pornography

⇨ taking, downloading, viewing or distributing sexual images of children

⇨ encouraging a child to perform sexual acts in front of a webcam

⇨ not taking measures to protect a child from witnessing sexual activity or images

⇨ inappropriate sexual touching of a child, whether clothed or unclothed

⇨ penetrative sex.

Both boys and girls can be victims of sexual abuse, but girls are six times more likely to be abused.

What are the signs that a child is being sexually abused?

Children often don't talk about sexual abuse because they think it is their fault or they have been convinced by their abuser that it is normal or a 'special secret'.

Children may also be bribed or threatened by their abuser, or told they won't be believed.

A child who is being sexually abused may care for their abuser and worry about getting them into trouble.

Here are some of the signs you may notice:

⇨ Changes in behaviour – a child may start being aggressive, withdrawn, clingy, have difficulties sleeping or start wetting the bed.

⇨ Avoiding the abuser – the child may dislike or seem afraid of a particular person and try to avoid spending time alone with them.

⇨ Sexually inappropriate behaviour – children who have been abused may behave in sexually inappropriate ways or use sexually explicit language.

⇨ Physical problems – the child may develop health problems, including soreness in the genital and anal areas or sexually transmitted infections, or they may become pregnant.

⇨ Problems at school – an abused child may have difficulty concentrating and learning, and their grades may start to drop.

⇨ Giving clues – children may also drop hints and clues that the abuse is happening without revealing it outright.

How do I report child sexual abuse?

It's best not to delay if you suspect a child is being sexually abused.

You can talk directly to the police or your local children's social services and this can be anonymous. You can also get advice or report your concerns anonymously to the NSPCC by phoning their free helpline on 0808 800 5000. Or you can report sexual abuse to the NSPCC via email or online.

If you are a health professional and suspect a child you are caring for is experiencing abuse or is at risk of abuse, you can seek advice from the 'named nurse' or 'named doctor' in your hospital or care setting.

The NSPCC has more information and advice about child sexual abuse.

If you are concerned about your own thoughts or behaviour towards children, you can phone Stop It Now! in confidence on 0808 1000 900 or email help@stopitnow.org.uk.

If you are a child and someone is sexually abusing you, you can get help and advice from ChildLine – phone 0800 1111, calls are free and confidential.

Who commits child sexual abuse?

People who sexually abuse children can be adult, adolescent or a child themselves.

Most abusers are male but females sometimes abuse children too.

40 per cent of child sexual abuse is carried out by other, usually older, children or young people.

Nine out of ten children know or are related to their abuser. 80 per cent of child sex abuse happens either in the child's home or the abuser's.

Boys are more likely to be abused outside the home, for example at leisure and sports clubs.

You may notice that an abuser gives a child special treatment, offering them gifts, treats and outings. They may seek out opportunities to be alone with the child.

Which children are at risk of child sexual abuse?

Children are more vulnerable to sexual abuse if they have already experienced abuse of some kind. Children who live in families where there is child neglect, for example, are more at risk.

Disabled children are three times more likely to be victims of sexual abuse, especially if they have difficulties with speech or language.

Children can also be at risk when using the Internet. Social media, chat rooms and web forums are all used by child sex abusers to groom potential victims.

See how to protect your child from abuse.

What are the effects of child sexual abuse?

Sexual abuse can cause serious physical and emotional harm to children both in the short term and the long term.

In the short term, children may suffer health issues, such as sexually transmitted infections, physical injuries and unwanted pregnancies.

In the long term, people who have been sexually abused are more likely to suffer with depression, anxiety, eating disorders and post-traumatic stress disorder (PTSD). They are also more likely to self-harm, become involved in criminal behaviour, misuse drugs and alcohol, and to commit suicide as young adults.

Child sexual exploitation

Children who have been sexually abused are also at risk of sexual exploitation, in which children are sometimes passed around a network of abusers for sexual purposes.

1 March 2016

⇨ The above information is reprinted with kind permission from NHS Choices. Please visit www.nhs.uk for further information.

Football abuse: from one lone voice to a national scandal

Two weeks after Andy Woodward told of his sexual abuse as a young player, English football faces the worst crisis in its history.

By Steven Morris

It began with the former footballer Andy Woodward bravely stepping out of the shadows to describe to *The Guardian* the sexual abuse he endured as a young player. Two weeks on it has spiralled into a scandal engulfing clubs and communities across the UK.

By Friday, 18 police forces were investigating leads from at least 350 alleged victims, the NSPCC children's charity was processing almost 1,000 reports to a hotline and one of the world's most famous clubs, Chelsea, was facing questions about whether it had tried to hush up abuse allegations.

> **"Two players at Newcastle United were among those who came forward this week. Derek Bell told *The Guardian* how he was groomed and violated between the ages of 12 and 16 by the convicted paedophile George Ormond, his coach at the Montagu and North Fenham boys football club"**

All those involved – police, football administrators, players and their relatives, children's charities, lawyers – are convinced it will not end here.

The former England striker and NSPCC ambassador Alan Shearer was the latest to express his shock at what has emerged and solidarity with those who had come forward.

"Over the last week I have been shocked and deeply saddened to hear of the abuse that colleagues, and in some cases former team-mates, suffered," he said.

"I have nothing but huge respect and admiration for all the players who are now coming forward, bravely breaking years of silence in a bid to help others. They've carried a terrible burden for too long."

Shearer sought to reassure parents of children who would be playing football this weekend that changes had been made.

"We can never be complacent but thankfully huge progress has been made in the last ten years when it comes to safeguarding. All clubs now have dedicated people tasked with keeping kids safe, but there's always more to be done."

He also made it clear he believed the scandal was likely to escalate. "As the weeks go on, it seems likely that there will be more people coming forward who suffered abuse within football, and they will need to be given our support so as they can get the help they need and should have had years ago."

Two players at Newcastle United were among those who came forward this week. Derek Bell told *The Guardian* how he was groomed and violated between the ages of 12 and 16 by the convicted paedophile George Ormond, his coach at the Montagu and North Fenham boys football club.

Ormond went on to become involved in youth coaching at Newcastle, where he abused player David Eatock, during the Kevin Keegan years in the 1990s. "I can still remember the look on his [Ormond's] face, how terrifying it was, and how his eyes were possessed," Eatock told *The Guardian*.

The former England, Manchester City, Liverpool and Tottenham Hotspur player Paul Stewart described in harrowing detail how he was abused by the late Frank Roper, a well-known youth coach in the north-west of England.

"He said he would kill my mother, my father, my two brothers if I breathed a word about it... and at 11 years old, you believe that"

"He said he would kill my mother, my father, my two brothers if I breathed a word about it," said Stewart. "And at 11 years old, you believe that."

Individual clubs including Newcastle, Manchester City and Crewe have launched inquiries into how they handled allegations of abuse, or coaches who had turned out to be offenders.

On Tuesday, the former coach Barry Bennell was charged with eight offences of sexual assault against a boy under the age of 14. The offences allegedly took place between 1981 and 1985.

The Football Association has launched an independent review, which will be led by the barrister Kate Gallafent QC, who specialises in human rights and sport.

The FA chairman, Greg Clarke, described it as one of the biggest crises in the organisation's history. Asked about claims that clubs may have tried to bribe players to stay silent about their abuse, he described the concept as "morally repugnant". He has promised that any club guilty of "hushing up" sexual abuse to protect their image will be punished.

That promise may be tested after the *Daily Mirror* revealed that the former Chelsea player Gary Johnson signed a confidentiality agreement with the club in 2015 in return for £50,000 after he alleged he was abused by the club's then chief scout Eddie Heath in the 1970s.

"I think that they were paying me to keep a lid on this," he told the *Mirror*. "Millions of fans around the world watch Chelsea. They are one of the biggest and richest clubs in the world. All their fans deserve to know the truth about what went on. I know they asked me to sign a gagging order and how many others are there out there?"

Chelsea has refused to comment on the details of the allegations, only saying that it has appointed an external law firm to carry out a formal investigation

into a former employee, and would pass those findings on to the FA.

"Chelsea has refused to comment on the details of the allegations, only saying that it has appointed an external law firm to carry out a formal investigation"

On Friday, Southampton, a club renowned for its youth system, said it had contacted the police after receiving information in relation to historical child abuse. It followed BBC interviews with two former players, Dean Radford and Jamie Webb, who said they were groomed and abused by a former club employee.

Police chiefs said there was no sign of any let up in the reports of abuse. By the end of the week Greater Manchester police said it had identified ten suspects after receiving reports from 35 victims. The priority for forces was to assess whether those named posed a present risk to children, and to deal with them before moving on to investigate historical abuse claims.

But the allegations emerging are not confined to football, or even to sport.

The National Association for People Abused in Childhood (NAPAC) said it had seen a tenfold increase in the number of adult survivors of child abuse registering for its support groups, rising from 10 registrations a week to 100 in the last three weeks.

The NAPAC chief executive, Gabrielle Shaw, said: "This is not just about football; huge numbers of people suffered abuse in childhood, within the family or institutions. Survivors often feel shame, pain and confusion about what was done to them."

3 December 2016

⇨ The above information is reprinted with kind permission from *The Guardian*. Please visit www.theguardian.com for further information.

New Premier League season begins ... but child abuse scandal hangs heavy over football

An article from The Conversation.

By Jayne Caudwell, Associate Professor Leisure Cultures, Bournemouth University; Belinda Wheaton, Associate Professor in Sport and Leisure Studies, University of Waikato, Louise Mansfield, Senior Lecturer in Sport, Health and Social Sciences, Brunel University London and Rebecca Watson, Reader in Sport and Leisure and Studies, Leeds Beckett University

THE CONVERSATION

The new Premier League football season kicks off this week, with record sums of money spent by top flight teams on new talent.

The start of this coming season marks the 25th anniversary of the Premier League, and in a campaign first, it will get underway with a Friday night game – with Arsenal hosting Leicester at the Emirates.

This season will also see players competing for places in the 2018 World Cup squad, which will take place in Russia next summer. All in all, it's set to be an exciting season, with Newcastle United, Brighton & Hove Albion and Huddersfield Town hoping to make their mark in the league after promotion.

But despite all the new season anticipation, football continues to be plagued by allegations of historical child abuse. This comes after a number of former players waived their rights to anonymity and talked publicly at the end of last year about childhood sexual abuse by former coaches in the 1970s, 1980s and 1990s.

In response to these reports, a hotline was set up by the NSPCC for footballers who experienced sexual abuse – and it received over 1,700 calls within three weeks of its launch.

Abuse widespread

To date, Operation Hydrant – the police inquiry into 'non recent' child sexual abuse – has received hundreds of reports of historic child sex abuse within football, with 328 football clubs, spanning all tiers of the game, currently involved in the inquiry.

Statistics released recently by the operation show that the number of victims now stands at 741, with more than 270 suspects identified. Of those victims, 96% are male, and were aged between four and 20 years old when the alleged abuse took place.

While the vast majority of referrals relate to football, a number of other sports have also been referenced in the inquiry, including basketball, rugby, gymnastics, martial arts, tennis, wrestling, golf, sailing, athletics, cricket and swimming.

Since November last year, when the issue of child sexual abuse in football first gained public attention, cases have progressed through the legal system. This has led to the identification of individual men and the successful charge of indecent assault and sex offences.

It has also been revealed that some of the identified coaches held positions at professional men's football clubs. Yet despite the ongoing public

Football abuse statistics

Figures released by Operation Hydrant in June 2017 indicate that:

- The number of victims of non-recent child abuse related to sports, primarily football, is now 741.
- 276 suspects have been identified.
- 328 football clubs have been implicated.
- 96% of victims are male.
- Age range of victims ranges from four years old to 20 years old at the time the abuse took place.
- Most cases relate to football but there have been 27 referrals outside of football, these include basketball, rugby, gymnastics, cricket, martial arts, swimming, wrestling, tennis, golf, sailing and athletics.

Source: National Police Chiefs' Council, 2017

outcry, the football authorities have been criticised for their lack of effort and transparency. At the end of last season, eight professional clubs had failed to respond to the national independent inquiry and were in jeopardy of disciplinary action, and imposed sanctions by the FA (Football Association).

Macho culture

Much of the shock and outrage at the abuse allegations and convictions comes from the fact that the victims are men. Stereotypically, child sexual abuse in sport has been seen as being about male perpetrators and female victims. But the recent cases have shattered this myth, revealing that boys and men experience sexual abuse, too.

Undoubtedly, this stereotype acted as an obstacle for men to speak out about sexual abuse, because of the misconception that 'real' sports boys and sportsmen are not 'victims' of sex crimes.

This is hardly surprising, because since the early 1990s, feminist research has exposed the often damaging connections between masculinity and sport. Football locker rooms and clubs are traditionally very masculine and male environments, and evidence has shown that expectations of how male sports stars should and should not behave can demean, devalue and devastate the lives of individual athletes.

Position of trust

Paralympic athlete and crossbench peer Baroness Grey-Johnson has recently urged the UK Government to do more. She has recommended sports coaches be included as a "position of trust" within the Sexual Offences Act – which would prohibit a coach from having sex with someone who cannot consent. This is primarily used for the protection of young people who are above the age of consent but under the age of 18.

This builds on the work by Professor Celia Brackenridge on understanding and preventing sexual exploitation in sport. Back in 2001, her groundbreaking research exposed the extent and nature of abuse across many sports, and revealed the previously taboo subject of athlete abuse – including child abuse in football.

Brackenridge crucially offered practical guidance for athletes, coaches, clubs and governing bodies, and many sports organisations took her seriously and adopted athlete and child welfare programmes.

However, it was revealed last year that despite these guidelines being adopted by many clubs, in 2003, the FA made the decision to stop funding child protection projects meant to ensure children were safe from sexual abuse. The BBC's *Victoria Derbyshire* programme also reported that an evaluation of the project later suggested that some FA staff felt intimidated and unable to speak out.

Despite this environment of diminishing child protection and macho culture, male footballers did come forward – to speak out about the sexual abuse they experienced as children.

So as the Premier League's 25th season kicks off, and the national inquiry into historical abuse in football continues, work must go on to ensure justice is served. It is by tackling abusive behaviour swiftly and publicly, that the sporting world can help to safeguard against future abuse of boys and young men in football.

9 August 2017

⇨ The above information is reprinted with kind permission from *The Conversation*. Please visit www.theconversation.com for further information.

See it, say it, change it

An extract from the report by the Children's Rights Alliance for England.

Violence against children

This section of the report explores violence and neglect against children. It also looks at the use of force on children in school exclusion settings, during arrest and whilst being sectioned under the Mental Health Act.

The findings show worrying infringements of a child's right to be protected from all forms of violence (article 19) and failures to provide extra protection for children who do not live with their families (article 20). It also finds evidence of a child's right not to be subject to degrading treatment and punishments being breached (articles 37 (a) and 28.2).

Neglect, harm and abuse in foster care

Our research highlights particularly concerning issues for children living in foster care. As well as being denied rights to their own identity children are vulnerable to neglect and physical harm.

Children told us in foster placements where they didn't feel safe they felt the need to try and protect themselves, for example one child told us he "always used to sleep with a knife near me." (Male, 16)

One 16-year-old boy described his experience of neglect in foster care:

"With the carer as well as the social worker I was let down. I was left out. It was last winter I was there. I was left out in the snow for almost two hours, two and a half hours. I rung my social worker. Can't answer. I ring him in half an hour and 45 minutes. Then an hour. Then he still said 'I'm not a taxi service, I'm not coming to pick you up.' And I was standing there for two and a half hours. Wouldn't give us a key. Wouldn't give us a key to the house even though it was meant to be our home… For three years me and my sister stood outside the house till half five. My school was literally across the road. I was home by 3.25… Two hours I stood outside the house. No coat. Middle of winter. Snowing. Me and my sister." (Male, 16)

A 13-year-old boy described to us how his foster carer became angry and locked him out of the house at night in his pyjamas and without shoes:

"He locked the gate so I ran away. And he didn't even notice for about two hours I was gone… He was just on the sofa, wasn't even looking for me or anything…And it was really cold… I was in my pyjamas… And I saw one of my friend's mum… And it was two o'clock at night and she actually rung the police. And they just said 'Oh, you locked yourself out kid.'" (Male, 13)

In many examples children reported issues to social workers but were not believed, leaving them in situations where abuse continued to happen: "They didn't even believe me, they believed my carer. And he did it again the next day. And he just kept doing it." (Male, 13)

This left children in foster care living in situations of risk and fear: "You shouldn't be put in them situations… You shouldn't have to be scared." (Male, 16)

Another child described how when he was eight he was subjected to regular physical abuse in his foster home from a child the family had adopted previously:

"They had him from… at four months old I think adopted, he used to beat me up well bad all the time. And obviously because they were so protective over him that whenever social workers and that came round, it's 'oh, he does it to himself'… I started to run away loads, trying to run away back to the city where I grew up…" (Male, 15)

Children in foster care placements told us their foster carers did not pass on pocket money, or allow them money for clothing or basic necessities:

"She never bought us clothes. Never bought us food. Never gave us money for buses or transport to do anything." (Female, 18)

Other children said that after complaining they did get money but only £200 to cover four years of their life with foster carers.

Separated refugee children and children seeking asylum living in foster care also raised this issue:

"She told me, what do you do with the rest [of the money]?… and I told her, I'm just saving them up and I want to buy a phone. My birthday is coming and I want to buy a phone." (Male, 15)

In this case when the child came to access the money he had saved he was told: "that money is just for saving now" (Male,15) and never received it.

Some separated children told us they were unaware that they should be getting money and that their foster carers were taking it:

"… My weekly allowance, my money, she was not giving me. Because, I didn't know… she would just take everything and I didn't know anything, she was just taking everything." (Female, 16)

Violence in school exclusions, arrest and custody

School exclusion

Children we spoke to suggested that restraint is often used inappropriately in Pupil Referral Units and as a way to implement further punishments:

"I got put into a behaviour school and they used to put you in restraints like that and then if you used to struggle it used to leave burns on your arms and that and then if you struggled you went into a… a… isolation room." (Male, 15)

Arrest

Children in the focus groups talked about their experiences of being arrested and sometimes being subjected to intimidation. This included being driven around for unnecessarily long periods whilst handcuffed, and the police officers driving the vehicle discussing how the police station could be "rough". Children who had been arrested reported that force was often used unnecessarily even when they had been cooperating with the police:

"I didn't do anything, I was walking with them and they were dragging me." (Male, 16)

"I've been in my house before and pushed onto the sofa and both my arms behind my back and cuffed for no reason... if you'd just ask me I would have given you my hands myself but you've genuinely used force on me and there's no point. Look at me I'm tiny, why would you need to use force?" (Male, 16)

Children described experiencing pain when handcuffed. A 14-year-old boy told us how his hands were tightly bound behind his back one on top of the other causing him pain. Some children told us that the police tried to humiliate them when they were being arrested by commenting on their personal appearance: "you've got a big arse and stuff... you're short." (Male, 15)

The children we spoke to also described the threat of violence from police carrying Tasers as "really frightening" (Male, 17). A 17-year-old boy described the experience of having a Taser drawn on him and used on another child he was with:

"I just saw the little dot there and... I just went all warm, scared, I thought I'm going to get hurt now, I'm going to get a shock in a minute. They just stunned him and he was flopped on the floor. But the noise is mad, I don't like it, it scares me the noise." (Male, 17)

Children feel the police need to change the way children are arrested. One 17-year-old boy said at age 14 he was held for three days without charge: "I was sitting there for three days in a sweat box" (Male, 14).

Police detention and custodial settings

There are different types of custodial settings for children – Secure Children's Homes, Secure Training Centres (STCs) and Young Offender Institutes.

We spoke to children who had experienced these settings both for short periods of time whilst awaiting a court hearing and for longer periods after being sentenced. Children specifically highlighted issues relating to violence and abuse from staff in STCs housing children from 12–17:

"But yes, it's not a very nice environment, it's very corrupt. Staff bringing stuff in, it's not very nice. Even when you're getting restrained or something, staff always get cheap punches in and stuff like that, it's just what it's like... There's always someone there trying to put you down." (Male, 17)

Children who had been detained also identified physical abuse from other children as a big issue: "If you go in and you're very quiet you get beaten up, if you go in there and you're too loud you're going to get beaten up." (Male, 17)

These issues were identified as leading to self-harm, depression, anxiety and in an extreme circumstance, attempted suicide:

"There was a kid that tried pegging himself when he was in there. He did hang himself but he didn't die. And another kid in the part I was in that was always cutting himself, punching walls with hands... it was just not nice." (Male, 17)

Children who had been locked up felt there was a lack of support for their well-being, describing teachers who were present during school hours as the "only people you can speak to and even when you speak to them they're not going to listen too much." (Male, 17)

There were concerning findings relating to a lack of support for younger children both during arrest and in detention. An 11-year-old boy described how the police did not give him a chance to make a statement but sent him to 'prison' calling him "a little robber". No one explained where he was going, why, or for how long he would be held. Arrival at the secure unit was distressing:

"I just heard lots of shouting of children.... and the one of them was crying and one of them was kicking the wall or banging their head on the wall..." (Male, 11)

Those who had experienced detention told us there is an urgent need for better staff and more accountability to reduce a sense of isolation for children inside:

"...More professional people that need to watch what goes on... Potentially it's that feeling there's someone there that could be approached... There's a massive sense of isolation." (Male, 17)

Violence used in sectioning under the Mental Health Act

Children who had been compulsorily treated under legal 'section' or had had contact with the police because of their mental health told us that sometimes their rights were not respected:

"The police, God, they can come and detain you whenever they want... I'm sure they can't but they do..." (Female, 17)

"I would love for the police to have more training, I would absolutely love it, it doesn't always come down to training, it comes down to the person and them not treating you like shit. And that's... you don't have to have training to do that, you can just be a nice person..." (Female, 17)

Children reported being held in handcuffs for up to two hours and being left in cells overnight without charge or referral to hospital. Some children also believed they had sometimes been placed under section in order to justify the use of restraint by the police who otherwise would not have had grounds for this to be used. Others told us they had not been given access to food or water:

"I was in a police car for six hours, they didn't feed me". (Male, 17)

Children said they felt the police often used an unreasonable amount of force when placing them under arrest or section and said that the approach of police must be improved:

"I totally understand why the Mental Health Act is there I just think that sometimes they should weigh up whether it's detrimental to the patient before they go in all guns blazing." (Male, 17)

"Get young people to train police officers more around mental health. I don't expect police officers that are going to arrest you to give you a therapy session but they need to learn to respect boundaries". (Male, 17)

"I think that the police need to realise that underneath, when they're not in uniforms, they're human beings too. I think that they get a bit too authority... it's not like we've committed a crime or anything... it's not like you're a criminal and its not like you're a victim of crime; you just need someone there..." (Female, 17)

2016

⇨ The above information is reprinted with kind permission from the Children's Rights Alliance for England (CRAE). Please visit www.crae.org.uk for further information.

Poor children returning to school 'malnourished' following increase in 'school holiday hunger'

Around a third of children in the UK qualify for free school meals during term-time, but poorer families are increasingly struggling to feed them during holidays say teachers.

By Rachael Pells

The number of poor children going hungry during the school holidays is increasing to "heart-breaking" levels, teachers across the country have warned.

As many as four in five staff (80 per cent) reported a rise in 'holiday hunger' over the past two years, with parents of children who qualify for free school meals (FSM) during term-time struggling to find the money to fund extra meals during school holidays.

In a survey led by the National Union of Teachers (NUT), 78 per cent of the 600 teachers polled said they recognised children arriving at school hungry.

More than a third (37 per cent) went as far as to say pupils were returning after the school holidays showing signs of malnutrition.

Kevin Courtney, NUT general secretary, said: "These are heart-breaking findings which lay bare the terrible impact of poverty on the lives and educational experiences of many children.

"This situation should not be tolerated at all, let alone be allowed to persist in the sixth richest economy in the world."

Government figures show there were four million children living in poverty in the UK in 2014–15, an increase of 200,000 on the previous year.

This means around a third of children, or nine pupils in every classroom, should be eligible for free school meals.

Just 15 per cent of respondents said they were aware of initiatives run locally – for instance by the local authority or by charity groups – to help tackle hunger during school holidays.

Responding to the survey, one teacher said: "A large number of pupils are consistently hungry, not just in the holidays. Weekends are a particularly worrying time for pupils and a large number of pupils have just one main meal a day (school lunch)."

Another said: "It's heart-breaking to hear children not wanting holidays because they don't get to eat enough".

"Hunger in school-children has become more apparent over my seven years of teaching," said a third, "in particular children arriving at school having had no breakfast."

Around seven in ten (69 per cent) of teachers said that pupils' social well-being was negatively affected by holiday hunger, while more than half (57 per cent) of those surveyed said their physical health was impacted.

Almost three-quarters (73 per cent) said that their pupils' education was being negatively affected as a consequence of holiday hunger.

Mr Courtney added: "Teachers are working hard to achieve the best outcomes for their pupils but the challenges they face as a result of poverty are increasing, not diminishing, under this Government.

"The Government needs to take urgent action and adopt a serious poverty reduction strategy, including the implementation of universal free school meals for all primary children and measures to tackle holiday hunger."

17 April 2017

⇨ The above information is reprinted with kind permission from *The Independent*. Please visit www.independent.co.uk for further information.

© independent.co.uk 2017

Fabricated or induced illness

Fabricated or induced illness (FII) is a rare form of child abuse. It occurs when a parent or carer, usually the child's biological mother, exaggerates or deliberately causes symptoms of illness in the child.

FII is also known as 'Munchausen's syndrome by proxy' (not to be confused with Munchausen's syndrome, where a person pretends to be ill or causes illness or injury to themselves).

Signs of fabricated or induced illness

FII covers a wide range of symptoms and behaviours involving parents seeking healthcare for a child. This ranges from extreme neglect (failing to seek medical care) to induced illness.

Behaviours in FII include a mother or other carer who:

⇨ persuades healthcare professionals that their child is ill when they're perfectly healthy

⇨ exaggerates or lies about their child's symptoms

⇨ manipulates test results to suggest the presence of illness – for example, by putting glucose in urine samples to suggest the child has diabetes

⇨ deliberately induces symptoms of illness – for example, by poisoning her child with unnecessary medication or other substances.

How common is FII?

It's difficult to estimate how widespread FII is because many cases may go unreported or undetected.

One study published in 2000 estimated 89 cases of FII in a population of 100,000 over a two-year period. However, it's likely that this figure underestimates the actual number of cases of FII.

FII can involve children of all ages, but the most severe cases are usually associated with children under five.

In more than 90% of reported cases of FII, the child's mother is responsible for the abuse. However, there have been cases where the father, foster parent, grandparent, guardian, or a healthcare or childcare professional was responsible.

Why does fabricated or induced illness occur?

The reasons why FII occurs aren't fully understood. In cases where the mother is responsible, it could be that she enjoys the attention of playing the role of a 'caring mother'.

A large number of mothers involved in FII have borderline personality disorders characterised by emotional instability, impulsiveness and disturbed thinking.

Some mothers involved in FII have so-called 'somatoform disorders', where they experience multiple, recurrent physical symptoms. A proportion of these mothers also have Munchausen's syndrome.

Some carers have unresolved psychological and behavioural problems, such as a history of self-harming, or drug or alcohol misuse. Some have experienced the death of another child.

There have also been several reported cases where illness was fabricated or induced for financial reasons – for example, to claim disability benefits.

How a case is managed

The child

The first priority is to protect the child and restore them to good health. This may involve removing the child from the care of the person responsible. If the child is in hospital, the parent or carer may need to be removed from the ward.

The child may need help returning to a normal lifestyle, including going back to school. Younger children and babies who don't understand they were victims of abuse often make a good recovery once the abuse stops.

Older children, particularly those who've been abused for many years, will have more complex problems. For example, many affected children believe they're really ill. They need help and support to develop a more realistic understanding of their health. They may also need to learn how to tell the difference between the impaired perception of their parent or carer and reality.

It's common for older children to feel loyal to their parent or carer, and a sense of guilt if that person is removed from the family.

The parent or carer

Once the child is safe, it may be possible to treat the parent or carer's underlying psychological problems. This may include a combination of:

⇨ intensive psychotherapy

⇨ family therapy.

The aim of psychotherapy is to uncover and resolve the issues that caused the person to fabricate or induce illness in their child.

Family therapy aims to resolve any tensions within the family, improve parenting skills and attempt to repair the relationship between the parent or carer and the child.

In more severe cases, the parent or carer may be compulsorily detained in a psychiatric ward under the Mental Health Act so their relationship with their child can be closely monitored.

Parents or carers involved in FII are difficult to treat because most don't admit their deceptions and refuse to recognise their abusive behaviour. Therefore, in many cases, the child is permanently removed from their care.

The best results occur in cases where the parent or carer:

⇨ understands and acknowledges the harm they've caused

⇨ is able to communicate the underlying motivations and needs that led them to fabricate or cause illness

⇨ is able to work together with healthcare and other professionals.

Media controversy

There has been controversy in the media regarding FII, with some commentators suggesting that it's not a real phenomenon.

However, a great deal of evidence exists to show that FII is real. The evidence of abuse includes hundreds of case files from more than 20 different countries, the confessions of mothers and other carers, the testimony of children, as well as video footage.

9 October 2016

⇨ The above information is reprinted with kind permission from NHS Choices. Please visit www.nhs.uk for further information.

First ever annual statistical publication for FGM shows 5,700 newly recorded cases during 2015–16

There were 5,700[1] newly recorded[2] cases of Female Genital Mutilation (FGM) reported in England during 2015-16, according to the first ever publication of annual statistics.

The FGM statistics[3], published today by the Health and Social Care Information Centre (HSCIC), also showed that there were 8,660 total attendances[4] in the same period where FGM was identified or a medical procedure for FGM was undertaken.

Women and girls born in Somalia account for more than one third (37 per cent or 810 cases) of newly recorded cases of FGM with a known country of birth. Of the total number of newly recorded cases, 43 involved women and girls who self-reported to have been born in the United Kingdom.

In 18 cases, the FGM was undertaken in the UK, including 11 women and girls who were also born in the UK. Where the nature of the UK procedures was known, around ten were genital piercings[5] (FGM Type 47 – piercing.)

The five- to nine-year-old age group was the most common age range at which FGM was undertaken. This equates to 43 per cent (582) of the total number of cases from any country, where the age at the time of undertaking was known.

Female Genital Mutilation Enhanced Dataset, April 2015 to March 2016, experimental statistics includes information gathered from acute trusts, mental health trusts, GP practices and community services within mental health trusts.

FGM has been illegal in the United Kingdom since 1985 and the law was strengthened in 2003 to prevent girls travelling from the UK and undergoing FGM abroad. It became mandatory for all acute trusts to collect and submit to the *FGM Enhanced Dataset* from 1 July 2015 and for all mental health trusts and GP practices, from 1 October 2015.

Today's report also shows:

⇨ 112 NHS trusts and 38 GP practices[6] submitted one or more FGM attendance record in 2015–16. Submissions are only required when there is data to report.

⇨ More than half of all cases relate to women and girls from the London

---

1 Figures over 1 million have been rounded to the nearest 10,000 and those over 100,000 have been rounded to the nearest 1,000. Figures under 100,000 have been rounded to the nearest 10. Figures under 1,000 are unrounded. Percentages are rounded to the nearest whole number.

2 Newly Recorded women and girls with FGM are those who have had their FGM information collected in the FGM Enhanced Dataset for the first time. This will include those identified as having FGM and those having treatment for their FGM. 'Newly recorded' does not necessarily mean that the attendance is the woman or girl's first attendance for FGM.

3 Data completeness varies from 22 to 100 per cent in the items discussed (see below). Data completeness also varies by submitter. Overall completeness for variables discussed: Date of Birth - 99.9 per cent known. Country of birth - 38 per cent known. Pregnancy status - 44 per cent known. FGM identification method - 67 per cent known. FGM type - 44 per cent known. Deinfibulation undertaken - 37 per cent known. Age range when FGM was undertaken - 24 per cent known. Country where FGM was undertaken - 22 per cent known. Both country of birth and FGM Type - 26 per cent known.

4 Total Attendances refers to all attendances in the reporting period where FGM was identified or a procedure for FGM was undertaken. Women and girls may have one or more attendances in the reporting period. This category includes both newly recorded and previously identified women and girls.

5 Figures for FGM Type 4 are rounded to the nearest 5 to prevent disclosure. For the remainder of UK cases, numbers were suppressed and include unknown categories and Type 4 cases of an unspecified kind.

6 The four FGM Types defined by the World Health Organisation (http://www.who.int) are: Type 1: Partial or total removal of the clitoris and/or the prepuce (clitoridectomy). Type 2: Partial or total removal of the clitoris and the labia minora, with or without excision of the labia majora (excision). Type 3: Narrowing of the vaginal orifice with creation of a covering seal by cutting and appositioning the labia minora and/or the labia majora, with or without excision of the clitoris (infibulation). Type 4: All other harmful procedures to the female genitalia for non-medical purposes, including pricking, piercing, incising, scraping and cauterization. While adult women may choose to have genital piercings, in some communities' girls are forced to have them. The World Health Organisation currently defines all female genital piercings as a form of FGM. The data item FGM Type 4 Qualifier allows users to specify that the FGM was a piercing. The FGM Enhanced Dataset includes two additional categories relating to FGM Type 3 and an Unknown value: History of Type 3: Current state where a woman or girl had FGM Type 3, but has since been deinfibulated. Type 3 - Reinfibulation Identified: Current state where a woman or girl has been closed previously, opened and is currently closed again. Unknown: When the FGM category could not be ascertained. It is acknowledged that even for experienced healthcare workers who frequently see women and girls with FGM it can still often be difficult to determine the type of FGM that had been undertaken.

NHS Commissioning Region – 52 per cent (2,940) of newly recorded cases and 58 per cent (5,020) of total attendances.

⇨ Self-report was the most frequent method of FGM identification, accounting for 73 per cent (2,770) of cases where the FGM identification method was known.

⇨ 106 girls were reported as being aged under 18 at the time of their first attendance, comprising two per cent of all newly recorded cases.

⇨ 87 per cent (3,290) of women with a known pregnancy status were pregnant at the time of attendance.

⇨ 90 per cent (1,980) of women and girls with a known country of birth were born in an African country. This breaks down as follows -– Eastern Africa 879 (54 per cent), Western Africa 414 (25 per cent) and Northern Africa 175 (11 per cent). 141 (six per cent) were born in Asia[7].

⇨ 145 deinfibulation procedures were reported. This procedure is often performed to facilitate delivery during childbirth.

Responsible statistician, Peter Knighton, said: "This is the first time that annual data have been collected and published to give an insight into the practise and prevalence of FGM in England. The resulting data will support the Department of Health's FGM Prevention Programme and improve the NHS response to FGM by raising awareness, enabling the provision of services and management of FGM, and safeguarding girls at risk."

21 July 2016

⇨ The above information is reprinted with kind permission from NHS Digital. Please visit www.nhs.uk for further information.

7   In total 241 NHS trusts and 7,640 GP practices were active at the start of the reporting period (1 April 2015, using the Organisation Data Service (ODS) organisation reference tables, extracted 16 May 2016. http://systems.hscic.gov.uk/data/ods/datadownloads). There are 177 NHS trusts and 664 GP practices registered on the FGM Enhanced Dataset collection system, representing 73 per cent of active NHS trusts and 9 per cent of active GP practices.

Rape, murder, forced marriage: what girls in conflict zones get instead of education

THE CONVERSATION

An article from **The Conversation.**

By Pauline Rose, Professor, International Education and Director, Research for Equitable Access and Learning (REAL) Centre, University of Cambridge

Education is life-changing for children and young people, but the power of education is systematically ignored in situations of humanitarian crisis – and never more than at present. This neglect is reflected in the tiny amount allocated to children's schooling in humanitarian responses: it involves only 2% of humanitarian funding. This neglect affects the lives of a generation of children and young people forever – once their education is disrupted it can never be retrieved.

Progress towards recognising education as part of a humanitarian response has been slow and the crisis has been worsening – resulting in millions more children and young people who are missing the chance to go to school. There are now more displaced people than ever before – and around half of refugees are children.

And while the media is focused on the plight of families whose lives have been ruined by conflict in Syria, in other parts of the world millions of people have spent many years away from home. Dadaab, in northern Kenya, is the world's largest refugee camp and has been in existence for more than 23 years. Strikingly, there are more than 10,000 third-generation refugees in Dadaab, born to parents who were also born in the camps. Yet, while inhabitants of the camps see the importance of education as the only thing they can take home, until recently there were no secondary school opportunities for the vast majority of young people there.

The World Humanitarian Summit in Istanbul must be a turning point in giving prominence to education for those caught up in conflict, for the sake of this and future generations of children and young people.

Adolescent girls suffer most

Adolescent girls' education journeys are being blocked in four key ways, as

NOT JUST GIRLS

156 MILLION

MEN ALIVE TODAY WERE FORCED TO MARRY AS CHILDREN

SOURCE: WITHOUT VIOLENCE

our new infographic shows. First, with just 13% of the extremely small pot of UNHCR education funding allocated to secondary schooling, it is no surprise that just 4% of the poorest girls in conflict affected areas complete secondary school. As a result, adolescent girls in conflict zones are 90% more likely to be out of school than elsewhere.

These girls are not only invisible casualties – they also often become targets. Unsafe journeys to school and direct attacks on school buildings mean that for many girls, most famously Malala Yousafzai, fulfilling their right to go to schooling means risking their lives.

Not only have attacks on schools increased 17-fold between 2000 and 2014, but there have been three times as many attacks on girls' schools than boys' schools in recent years. It takes just one day to destroy a school, but will take years to rebuild. In Syria alone, 25% of schools have been destroyed, damaged or occupied since the conflict started.

Even their journeys to school place young girls at risk of physical and sexual violence. More than half of adolescent girls in the Democratic Republic of Congo report experiencing physical violence. And while all the 51 countries affected by conflict since 1985 have reported sexual violence cases against adolescent girls, less than 4% of the funding requested by aid agencies accounts for programmes to tackle gender-based violence. In these situations, saving lives is inseparable from changing lives through education.

CHILD SOLDIERS

THERE ARE

250,000

CHILD SOLDIERS IN THE WORLD

SOURCE: WITHOUT VIOLENCE

Limited opportunities

Early marriage is also a frequent alternative to education in contexts of severely limited opportunities and unsafe journeys to school. More than half of the 30 countries with the highest rate of child marriage are fragile or affected by conflict. And the transitions can be sudden – there were 18 times more early marriages among Syrian refugees in Jordan in 2013 compared with 2011.

A lack of education can also result in girls being recruited to fight in armed forces. While figures are hard to come by, on one estimate, around 40% of child soldiers are young women. Once recruited, their lives are disposable, three-quarters of suicide bombers in some West African countries have been identified as young women. And military and terrorist organisations abduct young women: in Chibok, northern Nigeria, Boko Haram abducted at least 276 girls – at least 219 of them are still missing.

Education cannot wait

There is an urgent need to remove the obstacles facing adolescent girls on their journey to school. The shocking statistics presented here provide clear evidence of a problem that can no longer be ignored. Facing up to the problem needs to be accompanied by taking action.

The launch of the Education Cannot Wait Fund at the World Humanitarian Summit next week is a golden opportunity for world leaders to show their commitment to transforming the lives of children and young people for the future.

But realising change is not just about grand gestures at world summits. As commitments we have made together with others as part of the US First Lady's 'Let Girls Learn' Initiative highlight, change has to happen on the ground. Changing journeys of adolescent girls requires working together with communities to ensure they finally get the education they deserve.

20 May 2016

⇨ The above information is reprinted with kind permission from *The Conversation*. Please visit www.theconversation.com for further information.

Neglect and abuse in childhood could have long-term economic consequences

People who suffer neglect and abuse in childhood are much more likely to have time off work due to long-term sickness and less likely to own their own homes when they reach middle age than their peers, according to new research undertaken at UCL.

The study, which is published in US journal *Pediatrics* and undertaken as part of the Public Health Research Consortium, showed that the potential socioeconomic impact of child neglect and abuse may persist for decades.

The researchers found that neglected children often had worse reading and mathematics skills in adolescence than their peers, which could hamper their ability to find work and progress in the job market. These factors did not explain the poorer standard of living for those reporting child abuse.

The team followed the lives of 8,076 people from birth in 1958 until the age of 50 years, examining key socioeconomic indicators.

A person's economic circumstances at the age of 50 are important because this is close to peak earning capacity in the UK and poor living standards at this age can signal hardship and associated ill health during old age.

The research found adults who had been neglected in childhood were approximately 70% more likely to have time off work due to long-term sickness and not own their home at 50 years, compared to their peers who had not suffered from child abuse and neglect.

Also, the risk of a poor outcome was greatest for people experiencing multiple types of child maltreatment. For example, those experiencing two or more types of child maltreatment, such as both child neglect and physical abuse, had more than double the risk of long-term sickness absence from work, compared to those experiencing no child maltreatment.

"Our findings suggest that maltreated children grow up to face socioeconomic disadvantage. This is important because such disadvantage could in turn influence the health of individuals affected and also that of their children," said Dr Snehal Pinto Pereira (UCL Great Ormond Street Institute of Child Health), who led the research.

"As well as highlighting the importance of prevention of maltreatment in childhood, our research identified poor reading and mathematics skills as a likely connecting factor from child neglect to poor adult outcomes. This suggests that action is needed to improve and support these abilities in neglected children."

According to a study in 2011 for the Department of Work and Pensions, Britain loses 140 million working days a year through sickness absence, while UK employers pay £9 billion a year in sick-pay-associated costs.

19 December 2016

⇨ The above information is reprinted with kind permission from University College London. Please visit www.ucl.ac.uk for further information.

Abused children more likely to be seriously ill as adults, says report

Public Health Wales study finds children who suffer abuse, violence or other trauma more likely to develop chronic disease.

By Steven Morris

Children who suffer abuse, violence or other trauma at home are more likely to become seriously ill as adults, a report has concluded.

The study says children who endure four or more adverse childhood experiences (ACEs) are more than twice as likely to be diagnosed with a chronic disease in later life compared with those who have experienced none.

They are four times more likely to develop type 2 diabetes, three times more likely to develop heart disease and three times more likely to develop respiratory disease, according to the report from Public Health Wales.

According to the report, over a 12-month period those with four or more ACEs were three times more likely to have attended accident and emergency units, three times more likely to have stayed overnight in hospital, and twice as likely to have visited their GP, again compared with people who report no ACEs.

The report, the first nationwide study of its kind produced by a public health body in the UK, argues that the reasons are not simply cyclical – that a child who has a challenging home life, where, for example, adults smoke or drink heavily, is more likely to do the same and suffer bad health as a consequence.

It points out there is growing evidence that in addition early life trauma leads to changes in neurological, immunological and hormonal development that have detrimental effects on health across a lifetime.

Children who are constantly exposed to stress can become permanently prepared to respond to further trauma – which can increase strain on the body.

ACEs are defined as traumatic experiences that occur before the age of 18, ranging from verbal, mental and physical abuse to exposure to alcoholism, drug use, domestic violence or parents' relationships breaking down.

The lead report author, Prof Mark Bellis, the director of policy, research and international development at Public Health Wales, said its previous research had shown that ACEs increase the uptake of health-harming behaviours such as smoking and drug use and reduce mental well-being in adults.

He said: "This report shows how experiencing abuse and other problems in childhood are linked with increased levels of chronic disease in adulthood and much greater use of healthcare. What happens to us as children can make our bodies develop differently, leaving them more vulnerable to conditions like type 2 diabetes and heart disease in later life."

Bellis said that finding solutions needed a change in approach. "This cannot be achieved by the NHS alone. That is why we are working with our key partners, including the Government, police, local authorities, charitable and voluntary sector organisations, to develop a joined-up approach to prevent ACEs and support adults whose health is suffering because of childhood trauma."

The relationship between ACEs and the development of health-harming behaviours and chronic disease in adulthood was first explored in the US in the late 90s. The Centre for Public Health at Liverpool John Moores University – now the Public Health Institute – ran the first British study in Lancashire in 2012.

More than 2,000 adults aged 18–69 took part in the Welsh study, providing anonymous information on their exposure to ACEs before the age of 18 and their health and lifestyles as adults. The results take into account socio-demographic factors and show it is not simply the children of 'deprived' homes who suffer ACEs.

Simon Capewell, the vice-president of the Faculty of Public Health, said the Welsh study was very important. "This is the sort of data that needs to be used to prevent health issues that become a burden on the NHS and on our society," he said.

> **"Experiencing abuse and other problems in childhood are linked with increased levels of chronic disease in adulthood and much greater use of healthcare. What happens to us as children can make our bodies develop differently, leaving them more vulnerable to conditions like type 2 diabetes and heart disease in later life"**

Wales' future generations commissioner, Sophie Howe, said the study showed public services had to work together. "This new evidence from Public Health Wales emphasises the importance of focusing on early years and reducing the number of children living in families where there is domestic abuse, mental health problems, substance misuse or other forms of abuse or neglect.

"If we don't tackle this we are storing up long-term health and social problems for these children and our public services further down the line."

1 November 2016

⇨ The above information is reprinted with kind permission from _The Guardian_. Please visit www.theguardian.com for further information.

Sexually abused children as young as 12 refused compensation on grounds they 'consented', warn charities

Hundreds of child victims refused payouts by Government agency since 2012, FOI figures reveal.

By May Bulman

Sexually abused children as young as 12 are being refused compensation by a Government agency on the grounds that they "consented" to their abuse, charities have warned.

The Criminal Injuries Compensation Authority (CICA) has refused payouts to nearly 700 child victims of sexual abuse since 2012, ranging between £1,000 and £44,000, according to a Freedom of Information request.

The charity coalition, which includes Barnardo's, Victim Support and Liberty, has written to the Justice Secretary David Lidington, demanding the Government urgently reviews CICA's guidelines.

While the law states that it is a crime to have sexual activity with someone under the age of 16, the payment rules are being interpreted to suggest children can consent to their abuse, the coalition said.

The charities are calling for the rules to be changed so no child groomed and manipulated into sexual abuse is denied compensation because they complied with their abuse through fear or lack of understanding.

YouGov polling for the campaign shows two-thirds of people (66 per cent) of people think the rules should be amended so a child cannot be found to have 'consented' to activities involved in their sexual exploitation.

In one case, a girl who was raped and sexually assaulted when she was 14 at the hands of a gang of older men who were subsequently jailed for 30 years was denied compensation by CICA on the grounds that "she had not been the victim of non-consensual sexual acts".

She was reportedly left devastated feeling that she was somehow responsible for the abuse she'd suffered.

Director of Liberty Martha Spurrier said it was a "disgrace" that a state agency could imply child sex abuse victims who may have been brainwashed or manipulated had.

"Grooming is brainwashing – perpetrators manipulate children into situations that look like consent. No child can consent to abuse, which is why the criminal law rightly says they are simply unable to do so," she said.

"For a state agency to tell children who have survived these horrific crimes that they did consent – and deny them compensation – is a disgrace. The Government must urgently change these guidelines."

Barnardo's chief executive Javed Khan called for the CICA's guidelines to be "urgently reviewed" to prevent rules that are supposed to protect children from harming them, saying: "For children to be denied compensation on the grounds that they 'consented' to the abuse they have suffered is nothing short of scandalous.

"The very rules that are supposed to protect children are actually harming them. The Government must urgently review CICA's guidelines so that young victims receive the redress they deserve. Ministers must guarantee that no child will ever be told that they consented to their own abuse."

18 July 2017

⇨ The above information is reprinted with kind permission from *The Independent*. Please visit www.independent.co.uk for further information.

Helping children recover from abuse

Many children suffering from the trauma of sexual abuse can benefit from a therapy using creative methods, according to a study by Durham and Bristol universities.

The therapy offered by the NSPCC, called Letting the Future In, gives children a chance to talk about their abuse experiences and to express themselves through activities such as painting, drawing and storytelling with a therapist.

The therapy sessions enable the children, aged four to 17, to safely work through past experiences and come to understand and move on from what has happened. The child's parent or safe carer is also offered individual sessions as well as joint sessions with their child.

Therapeutic support vital

In this largest ever trial of a sexual abuse therapy anywhere in the world, the researchers found that the Letting the Future In therapy worked particularly well in helping children aged eight and over recover from their experiences of sexual abuse. For younger children, those between three and seven years old, the study suggests the therapy may take longer to work.

Co-author of the report, Professor Simon Hackett from the School of Applied Social Sciences at Durham University, said: "Our study sends out an important message to children affected by sexual abuse and to their families. With the right help and support it is possible to recover and move on from abuse.

"Our study shows the importance of offering children and young people who have been sexually abused therapeutic support to deal with their experiences, but all too often children

are left to suffer the consequences of sexual abuse without professional help."

The Durham and Bristol study found that children over eight showed significant recovery from their experiences of sexual abuse after they completed the programme, compared with children who did not take part in the programme.*

Children under the age of seven showed good signs of recovery but only after they had taken part in the programme for a year or more, suggesting it takes longer for younger children to improve.

Lead author, John Carpenter, Professor of Social Work and Applied Social Science at the University of Bristol, commented: "Evidence-based therapeutic approaches are vital to help all children deal with the effects of sexual abuse. It is crucial that commissioners know which interventions work in 'every day' community-based services to improve outcomes for children, in a cost-effective way.

"This 'real world' evaluation of Letting the Future In is a significant contribution to the evidence base, providing benchmarks for others to evaluate interventions."

Impact of sexual abuse

Sexual abuse can have a devastating impact on children. Figures show one in 20 children in the UK have been sexually abused, yet only one in eight comes to the attention of statutory agencies.

Where victims are known, effective treatments and interventions are crucial to help children recover from their traumatic experiences.

Jon Brown, NSPCC Head of Development and Impact, said: "These findings provide promising

indications that the Letting the Future In intervention can significantly reduce the highest levels of trauma experienced by children who have been sexually abused. We know that professionals say support for children after abuse is inadequate. Over half say that tight criteria to access local NHS mental health services means these children are increasingly struggling to access vital help.

"This study shows that therapeutic work can be delivered by a greater range of professionals, including social workers who receive additional training in therapeutic work – as in the case of Letting the Future In."

Positive changes

Parents and carers who were interviewed were unanimous in thinking that the intervention had resulted in positive changes. They identified improved mood, confidence, and being less withdrawn, a reduction in guilt and self-blame, reduced depression, anxiety and anger, improved sleep patterns and better understanding of appropriate sexual behaviour. As many said: "I've got my child back."

The trial included 242 children and young people and their carers, with 74 per cent girls and 26 per cent boys. Two-thirds of those taking part were abused by someone within the family and most by a single perpetrator. Over half of the older children had experienced three or more types of victimisation in addition to sexual abuse.

Participating children were assessed at the start of the programme, after six months and again after 12 months, using a range of standardised measures which show their levels of trauma, and related symptoms such as anxiety and stress. Interviews were also conducted with practitioners delivering the therapy, and with children receiving it.

The Letting the Future In programme is currently offered by 20 NSPCC teams across England, Wales and Northern Ireland.

The study has shown promising evidence about what works to help children recover from the trauma of being sexually abused.

For those children aged eight and over, the proportion of children receiving the intervention who experienced the highest levels of trauma dropped from 73% at the start of the programme to 46% after six months.

Even taking into account those who failed to engage in the intervention, or who had dropped out early, the reduction was 68% to 51%.

There was no statistically significant change in scores for the waiting list control group in either analysis, so improvements can be attributed to receiving Letting the Future In.

The evaluation of Letting the Future In is one of a number of research projects conducted by the Centre for Research into Violence and Abuse at Durham University. The Centre is dedicated to improving knowledge about interpersonal violence and abuse and the driving force of the Centre's members is to prevent violence and abuse in society and to help those who have been victimised. Other projects are looking at domestic violence, rape and sexual assault.

* Children in the control group took part in the programme six months later.

22 February 2016

⇨ The above information is reprinted with kind permission from Durham University. Please visit www.dur.ac.uk for further information.

The time for a child abuse helpline is now

News that the Government has finally fulfilled its promise and launched a consultation into mandatory reporting and acting on child abuse and neglect is clearly a welcome move.

By Peter Garsden

This is already the law in most civilised countries around the world, including Ireland, but not yet in England and Wales. But why should we sit back and wait for the law to change when steps could be taken right now to help identify people who abuse those most precious to us?

Although a legal obligation for early years' practitioners and support staff in nurseries to report any suspicions of child abuse, where a failure to do so triggers a possible criminal prosecution may seem harsh, it could help ensure that these crimes are no longer allowed to be swept under the carpet. Early years' workers should by no means take it personally; what the law aims to achieve has immense significance, and far from seeks to criminalise professionals.

Mandatory reporting, rather, could empower staff to report any suspicions or evidence outside of line of management, directly to a third-party agency. Because although safeguarding policies are already in operation across the nursery world, history has taught us that abusers are determined and sometimes sophisticated in their tactics.

I am optimistic that this consultation will result in a change in the law. After having represented victims for more than two decades, it has been a long time coming. But we are talking about one of the most serious and sinister offences, and action to help uncover abuse against children cannot wait many more months and even years for potential proposals to become law.

Abusers have done well to keep their actions hidden so there is no exact statistic on how many children suffer abuse and neglect today. The National Society for the Prevention of Cruelty to Children has highlighted that there are more than 57,000 children identified as needing protection from abuse in the UK. The Department for Education has reported that more than half of the children who are currently in care have been taken in because of abuse or neglect. But sadly I fear this is merely the tip of the iceberg. For every child identified, another eight are estimated to suffer abuse. A sobering and saddening thought which in itself should have been enough to spur the Government into action years ago.

Speaking up

In the past two decades I've worked on several cases where the abuse was systemic and highly organised. I have seen cases where innocent members of public sector staff were silenced either out of fear of what might happen to them, or because they were afraid of what the abusers would do if they didn't keep quiet. There is sadly no reason to believe that this doesn't still occur and we need a simple and effective system for those people to safely and immediately report what they have seen or heard.

Unfortunately, there is also no reason to think that paedophile rings operating in institutional settings are merely a thing of the past. Career paedophiles are organised and persistent, and their actions do not happen in isolation. The nature of these crimes means victims often won't come forward for many years, which makes prosecuting the offenders extremely challenging. However, someone around them will know, hear or see something, and those people must have a safe and direct route for reporting it.

It is a fact that the more contemporary that child abuse cases are when investigated, the higher the chances are of a successful prosecution. There is a groundswell of support for a publicly funded and widely publicised child abuse helpline. Many states in America and Australia already operate such dedicated helplines; they are well-funded and expansive. It is my opinion that the UK needs to follow suit immediately.

Introducing the law of mandatory reporting is a start, but I would like to see a law that requires everyone to report suspicions or instances of child abuse immediately – not just public sector employees. This is an area that absolutely demands resources and focus from the Government without a delay.

8 August 2016

⇨ The above information is reprinted with kind permission from Nursery World. Please visit www. nurseryworld.co.uk for further information.

Involving children in decisions 'will help protect them from sexual abuse'

Research commissioned by royal commission on topic of child-safe institutions released.

By Melissa Davey

Involving children in the research and decisions that will impact their lives is essential to protect them from being abused within institutions such as sporting clubs, churches and schools, a symposium held by the child sexual abuse royal commission has heard.

On Monday, researchers released the findings from three research reports ordered by the commission on the topic of child-safe institutions. The reports examined: key elements of child-safe organisations; the safety of young people in residential care; and disability and institutional child sexual abuse.

One of the six royal commissioners, Justice Jennifer Coate, told the symposium that survivors of child sexual abuse often shared their stories in the hope they could help stop the scourge of child sexual abuse into the future. As children, they were often unheard, or heard but ignored and punished.

"A key challenge for the commission has been the lack of research on institutional child sexual abuse to date," Coate said. "There has been no large-scale, cross-jurisdiction focus on the topic."

To address this, almost 100 research projects had been commissioned involving 40 universities and research centres, she said.

Protecting children in care

Researchers from the Institute of Child Protection Studies at the Australian Catholic University, Professor Morag McArthur and Dr Tim Moore, shared their findings from interviews with 27 children and young people living in residential care in Australia.

The children were asked about what they thought might prevent sexual abuse, what helped them to feel safe, how well their concerns were responded to, and what could be done to increase their safety.

"Residential care felt most safe when it was home-like: where young people felt welcome, where things felt 'normal' and where adults looked out for them," the researchers found.

"Participants stressed the importance of stability and predictability in residential care: where children and young people knew what was going to happen, where they felt that they knew their peers and how to manage their behaviours and where tensions could be resolved. Due to its highly chaotic and ever-changing nature, many characterised residential care as being unsafe."

The researchers found routine, fair rules, an opportunity to have a say and a sense of control also helped children feel safe.

The researchers said much of the existing research relied heavily on the views of residential care staff and clinicians and on documents, but failed to consider the experiences of children.

"People are very worried about the vulnerabilities of children and that involving them might upset and re-traumatise them," McArthur told Guardian Australia.

"They also question children's capacity to be engaged in these discussions. But children are capable, they want to participate, and they are agents who are active in their own lives. If we don't understand how children see and experience the world, we won't respond adequately and that means we can't keep them safe."

The royal commission has previously found that although 4.7% of children in out-of-home were in residential care as of June 2014, 33% of child sexual abuse reports related to children in residential care.

Children with disabilities

New research was also presented about the prevalence and prevention of sexual abuse of children with disabilities in institutions. The research was led by Professor Gwynnyth Llewellyn from the University of Sydney's faculty of health sciences, and it too highlighted absence of child perspectives and ideas.

"Segregation and exclusion in closed institutional contexts away from public scrutiny leaves children with disability at heightened risk of violence and harm including sexual abuse," her report found. "Further, when children with disability are stereotyped as dependent and passive and unable to 'speak up', they are at heightened vulnerability to being segregated, abused, overlooked and not heard."

Llewellyn told the symposium that data about the extent of the abuse was woeful.

"Right now the abuse of children with disability in Australia is not being measured, and what is not being measured cannot be counted," Llewellyn said. "What cannot be counted cannot be monitored or evaluated."

Her evaluation found that while there were many existing studies describing the issue of sexual abuse of children with disabilities, such studies could not produce evidence-based solutions. They could only propose solutions, she said.

"There was much less research using study designs which test interventions or solutions or evaluate policy initiatives," her report said. "In other words, study designs that allow us to know what works, and ideally, for whom and under what conditions. Research that can determine what works and in which settings is urgently needed."

Llewellyn's report also warned against thinking about children with disabilities as a special, distinct group. Doing so implied responsibility

Do we get to have our say?

for special groups sat "outside" of mainstream services and that those services could therefore be "relieved" of their responsibilities to those children.

Child-safe organisations

Through its work over the past four years, the royal commission identified ten elements that were critical to making an institution safe for children. These elements included: child participation in decisions and a culture of taking children seriously; child-focused processes to respond to complaints of child sexual abuse; and the continuous review and improvement of child safety standards.

To check the veracity and feasibility of its findings, the commission asked the University of New South Wales social policy research centre and parent research centre to obtain independent feedback on the ten elements from a panel of 40 Australian and international independent experts.

This research, led by Dr Kylie Valentine, asked the experts how relevant, reliable and achievable the child-safe elements identified by the royal commission were.

The research found a high level of support for the elements if they were

implemented well, but concerns were also raised about the level of resourcing needed to implement them.

"They support mandatory and comprehensive implementation, but with the recognition... that some organisations that provide very important services to children and their families – for example, sport and recreation clubs and childcare centres – will in fact be poorly resourced and not able to support implementation themselves," the report found.

Valentine told Guardian Australia that it was also essential that children had the opportunity to opt out of research.

The research will help inform the royal commission's final report, to be tabled on 15 December, which will include a volume dedicated to making institutions child safe.

1 May 2017

⇨ The above information is reprinted with kind permission from *The Guardian*. Please visit www.theguardian.com for further information.

Failure to report child abuse could become a criminal offence

Early years' workers could be prosecuted if they fail to report their suspicions of child abuse or neglect to local authorities.

By Catherine Gaunt

Under plans put out in a joint consultation, the Department for Education and the Home Office are considering whether to make it a new legal duty for certain groups, professionals and organisations to report and take appropriate action when they know or suspect that a child is suffering, or is at risk of suffering, abuse or neglect.

The scope of either new duty could extend to organisations or practitioners working in education, childcare, social care, healthcare and law enforcement.

In the early years' sector this could include early years' teachers, nursery staff and childminders.

It could also extend to support staff and administrators, including school secretaries and caretakers.

The consultation is part of wide-ranging reforms that the Government is carrying out of the child protection system in the wake of high-profile abuse cases such as Saville, Rotherham and Rochdale.

The consultation *Reporting and acting on child abuse and neglect* outlines options for reform of the child protection system in England.

It seeks views on the possible introduction of one of two additional statutory measures:

⇨ a mandatory reporting duty, which would require certain practitioners or organisations to report child abuse or neglect if they knew or had reasonable cause to suspect it was taking place;

⇨ a duty to act, which would require certain practitioners or organisations to take appropriate action in relation to child abuse or neglect if they knew or had reasonable cause to suspect it was taking place.

Currently practitioners and organisations should follow statutory guidance, but as the consultation explains, statutory guidance does not impose legal requirements itself.

A joint foreword by the Home Office minister Sarah Newton and education minister Edward Timpson says, "High profile cases have led to calls for specific reforms to our child protection system. In particular, the introduction of a new mandatory reporting scheme or other measures focused on taking action on child abuse and neglect have been suggested.

"The issues involved are complex and the evidence for such schemes is mixed. We need to consider carefully all the available evidence and views of a range of experts, children, families, survivors and practitioners so that any changes we make to the system do deliver the best outcomes for children."

Mandatory reporting already exists in the United States, Australia and Canada. The document points out that the current referral rate in England of 54.8 per 1,000 children in 2014–15 is higher than the rate in the USA – 47.1 per 1,000 children in 2012-13 – and Australia, 37.8 per 1,000 children in 2013–14.

The consultation also sets out the possible benefits and risks of introducing these measures.

It says, "Any additional legislation needs to bring benefits and not create perverse incentives or unintended consequences. We want people to actively identify child abuse and neglect and not turn a blind eye. Practitioners need to concentrate in cases here the issues are genuinely concerning and be empowered to use their professional judgement and discretion."

It also considers the scope, accountability and sanctions of the two potential measures.

It proposes that if a practitioner had "reasonable cause to suspect" a child was being abused or neglected, they would be expected to take appropriate action under a duty to act or to make a report under mandatory reporting to local authority children's social care. This would apply the same level of trigger as is currently used for initiating a local authority child protection investigation under section 47 of the Children Act 1989.

Sanctions could apply at individual and organisational level. Individuals breaching the new measures could face fines and imprisonment, while for organisations' sanctions could include unlimited fines, remedial orders and publicity orders.

22 July 2016

⇨ The above information is reprinted with kind permission from *Nursery World*. Please visit www.nurseryworld.co.uk for further information.

© Nursery World 2017

Research shows smacking makes children more aggressive and at risk of mental health problems

An article from **The Conversation.**

THE CONVERSATION

By Raymond Arthur, Professor of Law, Northumbria University, Newcastle

It might be seen by some as one of the ultimate parenting taboos – to admit that you smack your child. Yet research from the Children's Society reveals just 14% of adults think slapping children is unacceptable. It's clear then that a lot of parents still see the odd smack as an acceptable form of punishment – for when all other methods of discipline have failed.

Many parents rationalise this type of punishment with the fact they too were smacked as a child and claim it didn't do them any harm. But did it?

Recently, researchers in the US examined over 50 years' of research involving more than 160,000 children and concluded that smacking children does in fact cause more harm than good. The researchers found smacking often "does the opposite" of what parents want and rarely results in increased immediate compliance by children. It was also shown that children who are smacked are more likely to exhibit higher levels of aggression and mental health problems as they grow up.

Smacking and the law

It is legal for a parent or carer to smack their own child in England, Wales, Scotland and Northern Ireland as a form of "reasonable punishment". This is despite the fact that current laws prohibit adults from smacking, pushing or shoving other adults – and also protect pets from violence.

Under the Children Act 2004, parents can smack their children provided it does not cause bruising, scratching or reddening of the skin. In this sense, the law limits the use of physical punishment, but it also sends out a dangerous message that it is legally acceptable to assault a child.

This is at odds with many of our European neighbours – 24 European countries have abolished parents' right to use any form of physical punishment. And yet unlike

Austria, Croatia, Denmark or Norway, in the UK parents can still smack or hit as a form of punishment.

Police, lawyers and prosecutors have the difficult task of deciding when hitting is hurting a child – both physically and mentally. The visibility of bruising is often used as a test of whether a smack has been too hard. But this is ineffective as different children have different colour skin and bruise in different ways. The current law also leaves things vague for parents, and makes it hard for them to know what degree of force (if any) it is okay to use.

Lasting consequences

An outright ban on physical punishment across the whole of the UK would be much easier to police. And it would also be consistent with the country's obligations under international law that children must be protected from all forms of physical or mental violence.

Technically, the fact that children can still be punished using physical and mental violence is in breach of the UN Convention on the Rights of the Child. This is something the United Nations has urged the UK Government to change – instead encouraging and promoting positive, participatory and nonviolent forms of discipline and respect for a child's equal right to human dignity and physical integrity.

Although at the time smacking can seem like a quick fix, it is clear it has long-lasting consequences. As the latest research shows, discipline involving the infliction of violence can be damaging to a child – both physically and emotionally. It is clear then that the legal acceptance of beating children must end, thereby putting the child in exactly the same position as adults and pets in respect of the law.

Ultimately, a ban on smacking would not only provide children with greater protection, but it would also let parents know clearly what is and isn't acceptable when it comes to disciplining a child. But beyond all this, it would also help children to grow up happier and healthier – and what can possibly be more important than that?

5 September 2017

How to help teenagers stay safe online

We often think of teenagers as being tech-savvy, but how much do they know about staying safe online? To mark Safer Internet Day on 9 February 2016, Jo Budden, editor of our LearnEnglish Teens website, took a look at the issues and offers some practical tips.

Many people think teenagers today are light-years ahead of most adults when it comes to using technology. Young people use their phones and tablets so quickly and naturally that it's easy to believe they know all there is to know about the online world. However, teenagers often have a lot to learn when it comes to staying safe online and knowing what to do if problems arise.

A recent survey from the National Society for the Protection of Cruelty to Children (NSPCC) revealed that one in four young people in the UK has seen something upsetting on a social networking site. Of these children, 58 per cent were upset by someone they only knew online. Only 22 per cent of the children who had a negative online experience spoke to someone about their problem.

These statistics highlight two important points. The first is that we must do more to encourage young people to talk about their experiences online if we are to keep them safe. The second is that a 'friend' means different things to different people in different contexts – online, the word takes on a whole new meaning. Many young people have 'friends' in their online networks that they've never met: these may be friends of friends or people who share a similar interest such as online gaming. But the fact is, in many cases, they don't really know who their 'friends' actually are. This can leave them in a very vulnerable position.

> **"A recent survey from the National Society for the Protection of Cruelty to Children (NSPCC) revealed that one in four young people in the UK has seen something upsetting on a social networking site"**

So whose job is it to help guide teenagers through the digital environment that has been a part of their lives since they were born? Experts in the area suggest that adults need to play an active part. Taking a back seat and assuming that young people instinctively know how to behave online can be very dangerous. Instead, parents, teachers and youth workers should bring up the topic of online safety with young people and take the lead in encouraging safe online behaviour.

Creating a contract between parents and children

Designers of a recently launched app called Our Pact have recognised that parents often need a helping hand with guiding their children towards safe online behaviour. The concept is simple: parents talk to their children about how they spend their online time and then sign a contract with them on the use of their mobile devices. The app enables parents to control the amount of time their children can access Wi-Fi and what apps they can use. The idea is to encourage a fluid dialogue between parents and children about their online use.

So far, the early adopters that I've read about and talked to seem happy with how it's working. To me, the recent launch of this app is a sign that parents are looking to tackle the topic with their children head-on.

Tips for helping learners stay safe online

As well as parents, teachers can also play a vital role in ensuring that teenagers get the most out of the Internet. This involves introducing all sorts of digital literacy skills such as how to search for information effectively, and how to assess the reliability of different sources.

Yes Sparky, I know who my real friends are!

The dangers of location-tracking apps

Recently, there has been a lot of debate about the safety of apps that track and reveal the user's location.

For example, there were concerns that the PokemonGo app could be used to lure children into dangerous situations via the PokeStop feature (anywhere can be turned into a PokeStop and users visit the location to collect more Pokemon).

The Twitter-linked app Periscope has also come under fire because it allows users to broadcast video in real-time, including their location. Potentially, this could be used by those aiming to groom vulnerable young people. Even more concerning is the fact that videos and locations are time-stamped, allowing the viewer to track the user's movements.

It's also useful to have some general principles or guidelines for learners when using the Internet, such as those we have developed on LearnEnglish Teens.

⇨ Be nice to people online

⇨ Take care with what you share

⇨ Keep personal information private

⇨ Check your privacy settings

⇨ Know how to report posts

⇨ Keep your passwords safe

⇨ Never meet anyone in person you've only met online

⇨ If you see anything online that you don't like or you find upsetting, tell someone you trust.

Activities and resources for encouraging online safety

These guidelines appear in a reading activity, a listening activity and a video, all of which have been designed for teenagers with lower levels of English. For those at higher levels, there's a longer reading text about online safety in the UK, a quiz which asks learners if they are good digital citizens, and a reading activity about digital footprints to encourage learners to take care with what they share.

Songs are a great way to capture young people's attention. To celebrate last year's Safer Internet Day, GMC Beats rap workshops worked with Webwise Ireland to create a brilliant song full of strong, online safety messages. LearnEnglish Teens has created online support materials and worksheets so that learners of English can also enjoy this song, which gives online safety advice and reminds us that the Internet is an amazing tool for learning and having fun.

The Premier Skills English website has some online material in a comic format that brings some of the more serious issues of online safety to light in a really original way. The comics deal with the issues of meeting people in real life that you've only met online, and also taking care with what you share online.

"If you see anything online that you don't like or you find upsetting, tell someone you trust"

However you choose to talk about online safety, it's never too early to start. LearnEnglish Kids is the British Council's learner website for 5- to 12-year-olds, and there are some online safety activities and a quiz to introduce clear online safety messages to younger children. There's also advice and tips for parents. Extra support for teachers is provided on the TeachingEnglish website. This lesson plan gives structure and guidance on how teachers could take the topic into their classrooms.

Any day is a good day for talking about online safety with the young people you live with or work with, so if you're reading this after 9 February 2016, don't wait for next year... talk about it today.

2 February 2016

⇨ This content was originally published in Voices, the Brisith Council's external online magazine, and is republished here with permission.

The 51 countries that have banned corporal punishment

Slovenia has become the latest country to ban corporal punishment in all settings, including in the home, after its parliament passed a law late last month amending its law on prevention of family violence.

This reform makes Slovenia the 51st state worldwide to fully prohibit all corporal punishment of children, the 30th Council of Europe member state, and the 21st European Union state to do so.

The new Slovenian legislation entered into force on 19 Nov.

The UN Committee on the Rights of the Child defines corporal punishment as "any punishment in which physical force is used and intended to cause some degree of pain or discomfort, however slight", and it calls physical punishment "invariably degrading".

Corporal punishment in schools is banned in 128 states but only 10 percent of children worldwide are protected by laws banning corporal punishment at home and in school.

Sweden was the world's first country to ban corporal punishment in 1979. Besides Slovenia, two other countries – Mongolia and Paraguay – enacted legislation this year banning corporal punishment in all settings.

A full list of countries that have enacted laws prohibiting violence against children in the home and school is below, courtesy of the Global Initiative to End Corporal Punishment.

21 November 2016

⇨ The above information is reprinted with kind permission from the UN Tribune. Please visit www.untribune.com for further information.

© UN Tribune 2017

- 2016 – Mongolia, Paraguay, Slovenia
- 2015 – Benin, Ireland, Peru
- 2014 – Andorra, Estonia, Nicaragua, San Marino, Argentina, Bolivia, Brazil, Malta
- 2013 – Cabo Verde, Honduras, TFYR Macedonia
- 2012 – South Sudan
- 2010 – Albania, Congo, Kenya, Tunisia, Poland
- 2008 – Liechtenstein, Luxembourg, Republic of Moldova, Costa Rica
- 2007 – Togo, Spain, Venezuela, Uruguay, Portugal, New Zealand, Netherlands

- 2006 – Greece
- 2005 – Hungary
- 2004 – Romania, Ukraine
- 2003 – Iceland
- 2002 – Turkmenistan
- 2000 – Germany, Israel, Bulgaria
- 1999 – Croatia
- 1998 – Latvia

- 1997 – Denmark
- 1994 – Cyprus
- 1989 – Austria
- 1987 –- Norway
- 1983 – Finland
- 1979 – Sweden

"Be careful posting images online" is just another form of modern-day victim-blaming

An article from The Conversation.

THE CONVERSATION

By Anastasia Powell, Senior Research and ARC DECRA Fellow, Justice and Legal Studies, RMIT University

The revelations this week of yet another vile website where men and boys trade in the non-consensual images of women and girls has police and many in the broader Australian public concerned about these harassing behaviours.

Yet some of the media and public discussions of these image-sharing websites and forums also show a disturbing similarity to other examples of sexual harassment or violence against women.

Many, it would seem, are all too ready to shift the blame towards the victims. Advice circulating via various public statements, media coverage and school-based education resources repeatedly tells girls and young women to "be careful what you share" because these images will be "out there forever".

"Be careful what you share"

There are several problems with this kind of response.

Perhaps most importantly, such advice contributes to the shaming and humiliation of victims by placing the responsibility back onto them for their humiliation. Feelings of shame and humiliation are common reasons many victims give for not making reports to police about sexual forms of harassment and abuse.

The acting Children's eSafety Commissioner has called on victims in the most recent case to come forward with information to assist in what may be an international child-exploitation material investigation. So, avoiding sentiments that may further marginalise victims is particularly important.

Advice to victims "not to share intimate or private images" is also problematic. It obscures the variety of methods that harassers use to obtain images.

While little information is publicly available in this most recent case about the range of images and how they were all obtained, research suggests privacy of images is not always in the victim's control.

In ongoing research, my colleagues and I have found that, while many images of women and girls are obtained from public or semi-public social media accounts, many others are obtained illegally through hacking accounts and Internet-enabled devices, through 'upskirting' and 'creep shots', as well as through images originally shared privately with an intimate partner.

A further problem is that we seem to reserve a special kind of victim-blaming when it comes to sexual forms of violence, abuse or harassment. No-one ever told a victim of identity fraud that they should never have stored their money electronically in the first place, or how silly they were to make purchases online.

We seem to understand that cybercriminals exploit, trick and hack victims' information in a range

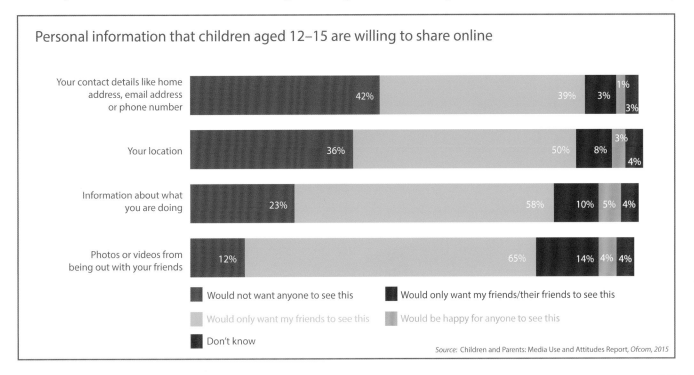

Personal information that children aged 12–15 are willing to share online

Your contact details like home address, email address or phone number: 42% | 39% | 3% | 1% | 3%

Your location: 36% | 50% | 8% | 3% | 4%

Information about what you are doing: 23% | 58% | 10% | 5% | 4%

Photos or videos from being out with your friends: 12% | 65% | 14% | 4% | 4%

- Would not want anyone to see this
- Would only want my friends/their friends to see this
- Would only want my friends to see this
- Would be happy for anyone to see this
- Don't know

Source: Children and Parents: Media Use and Attitudes Report, Ofcom, 2015

of ways to commit their crimes. We don't expect people to avoid all forms of e-commerce simply to prevent themselves from being victimised.

Yet last year, when nude images of hundreds of Queensland women were posted online, authorities reportedly warned victims about storing sensitive images on their digital devices at all.

A broader trend?

It is important to provide everyone with advice on how to protect their information online and to be aware of the potential for exploitation and abuse of their material.

But the line between providing advice and placing responsibility back onto victims is easy to cross. Often it lies in the balance of the messages directed to both perpetrators and victims.

How much of the media coverage comprises 'stern warnings' to potential victims as compared to potential perpetrators? How often are there calls for witnesses or bystanders to report their peers' concerning behaviour? What further information about common patterns in crime and violence, or how victims can get help, is included?

There are more positive examples. When nude photos of South Australian women were found to have been shared online last year, authorities took care to balance advice to victims on protecting their information alongside statements that emphasised:

"None of the women were to blame for the manner in which their stolen property had been used."

Yet research into media coverage of violence against women generally has repeatedly found that a majority of reports tend to focus overwhelmingly on the features of individual 'incidents' and the behaviours of victims, rather than in-depth coverage of the broader issues of gender-based violence with a focus on the perpetrators.

Crucially, the harms of such image-trading sites are not only in what the images contain, but also in how they are being used. From 'revenge porn' sites to 'blokes advice' pages to online forums designed to solicit creepshots and share identifying information about women and girls, there's a clear pattern in how those involved treat women as second-class citizens and mere sexual objects.

Particularly troubling is the 'pack mentality' of some online groups. Communities and localised groups that provide male peer support for sexual violence and abuse have been linked with higher rates of violence perpetration, for example.

The problem thus goes far beyond the trading in images (whether obtained from public sources or illegally) to broader issues of sexual and gender-based harassment of women and girls.

Some images that are not at all sexually explicit are likewise posted alongside women's identifying information. This encourages others to engage in stalking, voyeurism and/or account-hacking in order to contribute further images. Our research has found these associated behaviours can be very dangerous. In some cases, they have been linked to further targeted harassment of individual women.

Take away the images, regardless of how they were originally obtained, and we still have a social problem that no amount of advice to victims is going to solve.

19 August 2016

⇨ The above information is reprinted with kind permission from *The Conversation*. Please visit www.theconversation.com for further information.

System failing child sex abuse victims

In a report by the Children's Commissioner for England it has been alleged that victims of child sex abuse are being let down by the very systems and procedures that are designed to protect them from harm.

The findings highlighted that warning signs are being missed, investigations are being delayed unnecessarily and, perhaps most concerning of all, abused young people have to wait for therapy and are not permitted counselling before taking part in traumatic court cases.

Responding to the findings, Peter Garsden, child abuse solicitor and strong advocate for the rights of abuse survivors, argues that with the recent increase in awareness of sexual abuse crimes there has to be a better understanding of how to help those who have suffered abuse at a young age.

Long investigations

The focal point of the report was how child abuse cases were investigated, with the overarching conclusion that an increase in reports of sexual offences is placing strain on police forces and is resulting in investigations into abuse cases taking longer than other crimes.

Using the latest Home Office statistics the watchdog found that the average length of time spent investigating child sexual abuse cases was 248 days, in comparison adult sexual abuse cases had a median investigation time of 147 days, over 100 days less than the average for cases involving children.

Even beyond adult abuse cases, abuse crimes involving children took longer to investigate that all other crime types.

The 248 days it took, on average, to record and charge a suspect is longer than in cases that related to drug offences (which average at 90 days), theft (73 days) and violence against a person (72 days).

Further analysis of Home Office data showed that in 25% of child sexual abuse cases, investigations took considerably longer than the average, with a quarter of cases in 2015/16 taking 393 days or longer to bring a charge.

Worryingly, investigations into child abuse cases have been increasing in time over recent years:

⇨ In 2013/14 the average length of investigation was 179 days;

⇨ In 2014/15 this figure sat at 236

⇨ and, the most recent figures, for 2015/16, suggest the average investigation lasts 248 days.

While these figures are increasing, the time taken to investigate other types of sexual offences has been falling year on year.

It could be argued that cases of child sexual abuse are more complex and thus require longer investigations – but even with this reasoning, it is clear that survivors of child sexual abuse are waiting longer to see their perpetrator face prosecution.

Failing to spot symptoms

In another report released by the Children's Commissioner for England, who published three investigations simultaneously, it was found that young people are often left to report abuse themselves as authorities miss the warning signs of abuse.

In a report that focused on children's experience when seeking help and support after sexual abuse in the family environment, the Commissioner found that many abuse survivors faced long waits for therapy and were often blocked from having counselling before court cases.

Even in instances where victims did access counselling services, they were often forced to attend on their own, with family members not able or encouraged to join sessions; many respondents to the investigation explained that they felt it would have been beneficial for some family members to attend sessions alongside them, so that they had a better understanding of how they were feeling.

A third report from the Commissioner highlighted the role of schools in preventing child sexual abuse; this revealed that many teachers claim that they are confident that they would be able to spot the signs of abuse; however, as schools do not educate children about seeking help they do not fulfil their potential in preventing child sexual abuse.

Supporting survivors

Discussing the main findings from the three reports, Peter said:

"These reports reveal some telling figures about how child sexual abuse cases are investigated, how survivors are supported, and how schools are empowering children to seek help in these incidents.

"Most worrying is the length of time child abuse cases are taking to investigate, as throughout the prosecution process victims will be going through unimaginable emotional torment and for them to be waiting longer than any other crime victims to find out if their perpetrator will be brought to justice is hugely disconcerting.

"Likewise, it is very disappointing that children are still not receiving therapy and are being blocked from counselling before court cases, as this is probably the most stressful part of the process, where they will feel anxious about facing their abuser again.

"It is only right that children should be better supported through this process and with the increased understanding and awareness of these crimes, it's crucial that there's also a greater appreciation of the support that abuse survivors require when going through the process of prosecuting their abuser."

"We've been through the decades of abuse victims not being believed when they disclosed their experiences and in today's era, where we have increased awareness of the psychological effects of abuse, it is inconceivable that survivors are unable to access the support they need."

21 April 2017

How to spot child sexual exploitation

Each year in England thousands of children and young people are raped or sexually abused. This includes children who have been abducted and trafficked, or beaten, threatened or bribed into having sex.

Media coverage of police investigations into the crimes of Jimmy Savile and other prominent figures have brought child sexual abuse and exploitation to public attention.

But while police tackle the problem, child sexual exploitation continues to happen every day. It's important to understand what child sexual exploitation is and to be aware of warning signs that may indicate a child you know is being exploited.

What is child sexual exploitation?

Before explaining child sexual exploitation, it is helpful to understand what is meant by the age of consent (the age at which it is legal to have sex). This is 16 for everyone in the UK. Under the age of 16, any sort of sexual touching is illegal.

It is illegal to take, show or distribute indecent photographs of children, or to pay or arrange for sexual services from children.

It is also against the law if someone in a position of trust (such as a teacher) has sex with a person under 18 that they have responsibility for.

Child sexual exploitation is when people use the power they have over young people to sexually abuse them. Their power may result from a difference in age, gender, intellect, strength, money or other resources.

People often think of child sexual exploitation in terms of serious organised crime, but it also covers abuse in relationships and may involve informal exchanges of sex for something a child wants or needs, such as accommodation, gifts, cigarettes or attention. Some children are 'groomed' through 'boyfriends' who then force the child or young person into having sex with friends or associates.

Sexual abuse covers penetrative sexual acts, sexual touching, masturbation and the misuse of sexual images – such as on the Internet or by mobile phone.

Part of the challenge of tackling child sexual exploitation is that the children and young people involved may not understand that non-consensual sex (sex they haven't agreed to) or forced sex – including oral sex – is rape.

Which children are affected?

Any child or young person can be a victim of sexual exploitation, but children are believed to be at greater risk of being sexually exploited if they:

⇨ are homeless

⇨ have feelings of low self-esteem

⇨ have had a recent bereavement or loss

⇨ are in care

⇨ are a young carer.

"If you suspect that a child or young person has been or is being sexually exploited, the NSPCC recommends that you do not confront the alleged abuser. Confronting them may place the child in greater physical danger and may give the abuser time to confuse or threaten them into silence"

However, there are many more ways that a child may be vulnerable to sexual exploitation, and these are outlined in a report by the Office of the Children's Commissioner.

The signs of child sexual exploitation may be hard to spot, particularly if a child is being threatened. To make sure that children are protected, it's worth being aware of the signs that might suggest a child is being sexually exploited.

Signs of grooming and child sexual exploitation

Signs of child sexual exploitation include the child or young person:

⇨ going missing for periods of time or regularly returning home late

⇨ skipping school or being disruptive in class

⇨ appearing with unexplained gifts or

possessions that can't be accounted for

⇨ experiencing health problems that may indicate a sexually transmitted infection

⇨ having mood swings and changes in temperament

⇨ using drugs and/or alcohol

⇨ displaying inappropriate sexualised behaviour, such as over-familiarity with strangers, dressing in a sexualised manner or sending sexualised images by mobile phone ('sexting')

⇨ they may also show signs of unexplained physical harm, such as bruising and cigarette burns.

Preventing abuse

The NSPCC offers advice on how to protect children. It advises:

⇨ helping children to understand their bodies and sex in a way that is appropriate for their age

⇨ developing an open and trusting relationship, so they feel they can talk to you about anything

⇨ explaining the difference between safe secrets (such as a surprise party) and unsafe secrets

(things that make them unhappy or uncomfortable)

⇨ teaching children to respect family boundaries, such as privacy in sleeping, dressing and bathing

⇨ teaching them self-respect and how to say no

⇨ supervising Internet, mobile and television use.

Who is sexually exploiting children?

People of all backgrounds and ethnicities, and of many different ages, are involved in sexually exploiting children. Although most are male, women can also be involved in sexually exploiting children. For instance, women will sometimes be involved through befriending victims.

Criminals can be hard to identify because the victims are often only given nicknames, rather than the real name of the abuser.

Some children and young people are sexually exploited by criminal gangs specifically set up for child sexual exploitation.

What to do if you suspect a child is being sexually exploited

If you suspect that a child or young person has been or is being sexually exploited, the NSPCC recommends that you do not confront the alleged abuser. Confronting them may place the child in greater physical danger and may give the abuser time to confuse or threaten them into silence.

Instead, seek professional advice. Discuss your concerns with your local authority's children's services (safeguarding team), the police or an independent organisation, such as the NSPCC. They may be able to advise on how to prevent further abuse and how to talk to your child to get an understanding of the situation.

If you know for certain that a child has been or is being sexually exploited, report this directly to the police.

2 June 2016

⇨ The above information is reprinted with kind permission from NHS Choices. Please visit www.nhs.uk for further information.

© NHS Choices 2017

Key facts

- Child abuse can happen in different ways, and can include neglect as well as physical, emotional and sexual abuse. In many cases, people experience more than one type of abuse. (page 1)

- One in 14 adults was abused as a child in England and Wales. (page 3)

- About six million adults – aged 16 to 59 in England and Wales – are estimated by the Office for National Statistics to have experienced abuse as children. (page 3)

- Women are significantly more likely than men to report experience of abuse during childhood. The biggest difference is for sexual abuse: 11% of women reported some form of experience compared to 3% of men. (page 3)

- Up to eight per cent of males and 12 per cent of females experience penetrative child sexual abuse and up to 16 per cent of males and up to 36 per cent of females experience non-penetrative child sexual abuse. (page 7)

- The NSPCC states that there are currently over 56,000 children identified as needing protection from abuse in the UK. (page 8)

- A 2013 report by the NSPCC found that it takes 7.8 years (on average) for a child to open up to someone about sexual abuse. (page 8)

- Two weeks after former footballer Andy Woodward described the sexual abuse he endured as a young player… 18 police forces were investigating leads from at least 350 alleged victims, the NSPCC children's charity was processing almost 1,000 reports to a hotline and one of the world's most famous clubs, Chelsea, was facing questions about whether it had tried to hush up abuse allegations. (page 12)

- Figures released by Operation Hydrant in June 2017 indicate that:

  - The number of victims of non-recent child abuse related to sports, primarily football, is now 741.

  - 276 suspects have been identified.

  - 328 football clubs have been implicated.

  - 96% of victims are male.

  - Age range of victims ranges from four years old to 20 years old at the time the abuse took place.

- Most cases relate to football but there have been 27 referrals outside of football, these include basketball, rugby, gymnastics, cricket, martial arts, swimming, wrestling, tennis, golf, sailing and athletics. (page 15)

- As many as four in five [school] staff (80 per cent) reported a rise in 'holiday hunger' over the past two years, with parents of children who qualify for free school meals (FSM) during term-time struggling to find the money to fund extra meals during school holidays. (page 18)

- One study published in 2000 estimated 89 cases of Fabricated or Induced Illness (FII) in a population of 100,000 over a two-year period. However, it's likely that this figure underestimates the actual number of cases of FII. (page 19)

- There were 5,700 newly recorded cases of Female Genital Mutilation (FGM) reported in England during 2015-16, according to the first ever publication of annual statistics. (page 20)

- Self-report is the most frequent method of FGM identification, accounting for 73 per cent (2,770) of cases where the FGM identification method was known. (page 21)

- 156 million men alive today were forced to marry as children. (page 21)

- There are 250,000 child soldiers in the world. (page 22)

- Under the Children Act 2004, parents can smack their children provided it does not cause bruising, scratching or reddening of the skin. In this sense, the law limits the use of physical punishment. (page 31)

- Recently, researchers in the US examined over 50 years' of research involving more than 160,000 children and concluded that smacking children does in fact cause more harm than good. (page 30)

- A recent survey from the National Society for the Protection of Cruelty to Children (NSPCC) revealed that one in four young people in the UK has seen something upsetting on a social networking site. Of these children, 58 per cent were upset by someone they only knew online. Only 22 per cent of the children who had a negative online experience spoke to someone about their problem. (page 32)

- In 25% of child sexual abuse cases, investigations took considerably longer than the average, with a quarter of cases in 2015/16 taking 393 days or longer to bring a charge. (page 37)

Child abuse

The emotional, physical or sexual mistreatment of a child.

Child Protection Plan

A plan detailing what must be done to promote a child's development and health along with protecting them from further harm.

Child marriage

Where children, often before they have reached puberty, are given to be married – often to a person many years older.

Faith-based abuse

Child abuse or other crimes that can be linked to faith, religion or belief.

Female genital mutilation (FGM)

FGM is a non-medical cultural practice that involves partially or totally removing a girl or woman's external genitalia.

Grooming

Actions that are deliberately performed in order to encourage a child to engage in sexual activity. For example, offering friendship and establishing an emotional connection, buying gifts, etc.

In need

If the quality of a child's health or development is likely to be impaired unless provided by a local authority.

Internet Watch Foundation

A charity that works to minimise the availability of child abuse images and other criminal adult content on the Internet.

Legislation

A law or body of laws that aim to regulate behaviours or actions.

Mandatory reporting

The reporting of a crime or criminal behaviour that is required by law.

Neglect (emotional and physical)

A failure to sufficiently care for the needs of something or someone.

Physical abuse

Physical abuse involves the use of violence or force against a victim and can including hitting, slapping, kicking, pushing, strangling or other forms of violence. Physical assault is a crime and the police have the power to protect victims, but in a domestic violence situation it can sometimes take a long time for the violence to come to light. Some victims are too afraid to go to the police, believe they can reform the abuser (who they may still love), or have normalised their abusive situation and do not realise they can get help.

Sarah's Law

Campaigned for after the murder of Sarah Payne, the scheme allows parents to enquire about a named individual to establish whether they are a known sex-offender. Also called the Child Sex Offender Disclosure Scheme.

Sexual abuse

Sexual abuse occurs when a victim is forced into a sexual act against their will, through violence or intimidation. This can include rape. Sexual abuse is always a crime, no matter what the relationship is between the victim and perpetrator.

Assignments

Brainstorming

⇨ Brainstorm what you know about child abuse:

- What kind of things come under the definition of child abuse?

- What are some of the organisations who help victims of child abuse?

Research

⇨ Research the issue of 'school holiday hunger' and write a one-page report suggesting what could be done to help solve this problem. Start with the article on page 18 and then use the Internet for further research.

⇨ Research fabricated or induced illness, also known as Munchausen's By Proxy. Find at least two case studies and share with your class.

Design

⇨ Design a leaflet drawing attention to the issue of FGM. Include some statistics.

⇨ Choose an article from this book and design an illustration that highlights its key message.

⇨ Design an app that will allow students to gain confidential advice about child abuse.

⇨ In small groups, choose one of the types of child abuse discussed in the article on page four and create a poster illustrating the main characteristics of this type of abuse.

⇨ Create a leaflet that will be distributed to parents of children aged 11–13 advising how they can help keep their children safe online.

Oral

⇨ In pairs, discuss the issue of 'neglect'. Write down some examples of neglectful behaviour and then consider the effects that each behaviour might have on a child. For example, failing to keep a child clean and clothed is considered neglectful behaviour and could affect that child's health and experiences at school. Share your ideas with the rest of your class.

⇨ Social media sites like Facebook make it very easy for people to pretend to be someone they are not. Although there are age-restrictions on Facebook accounts, many children under 12 still manage to create profiles. Create a presentation aimed at 10- to 12-year-olds that explains Internet-based 'Stranger Danger'. Think carefully about how you can highlight the risks in a way that is engaging and age-appropriate.

⇨ Imagine that you volunteer for a charity such as ChildLine. You receive a call from a 12-year-old boy who is worried that his friend is being neglected. He says that his friend regularly arrives at school in dirty clothes and is always hungry. What would you advise your caller to do? Discuss your answer in pairs or small groups.

⇨ As a class, discuss the reasons children may stay quiet about abuse they have experienced.

⇨ 'Failure to report child abuse should become a criminal offence'. Debate this statement as a class, with half of you arguing in favour and half arguing against.

⇨ Choose one of the illustrations from this book and, in pairs, discuss why you think the artist chose to portray the issue the way he did.

Reading/Writing

⇨ Using the information from this book, write a short paragraph summarising the definition of 'child abuse'.

⇨ Write a two-page article on the use of social media and how it can increase the risk of child abuse.

⇨ Imagine you work for a charity which campaigns against child marriage in the UK. Write a blog-post for your charity's website explaining the issues surrounding child marriage and your feelings about the issue.

⇨ Imagine that you are the head master/mistress of a secondary school in the UK. You are concerned about the issue of child sexual exploitation and decide to write a letter that will be sent home to parents, warning them of the issue. Create a draft of this letter, explaining child sexual exploitation and the warning signs. You should also include advise on where parents can go for help and support if they are worried about their son/daughter.

⇨ Write an article for your school/college newspaper explaining why it is important to seek help if you have been sexually abused. Include some information about charities and centres that can help.

⇨ Write a summary of the article *Abused children more likely to be seriously ill as adults*, says report for your school newspaper.

Acknowledgements

The publisher is grateful for permission to reproduce the material in this book. While every care has been taken to trace and acknowledge copyright, the publisher tenders its apology for any accidental infringement or where copyright has proved untraceable. The publisher would be pleased to come to a suitable arrangement in any such case with the rightful owner.

Images

All images courtesy of iStock except pages 11 and 14: Pixabay, and page 36: Unsplash.

Icons

Icons on pages 21 and 22 were made by Freepik from www.flaticon.com.

Illustrations

Don Hatcher: pages 9 & 32. Simon Kneebone: pages 13 & 38. Angelo Madrid: pages 18 & 29.

Additional acknowledgements

Editorial on behalf of Independence Educational Publishers by Cara Acred.

With thanks to the Independence team: Shelley Baldry, Tina Brand, Sandra Dennis, Jackie Staines and Jan Sunderland.

Cara Acred

Cambridge, September 2017